Greetings from
Buchanan, Michigan

By

Leo J. Goodsell and Robert C. Myers

Berrien County Historical Association
Berrien Springs, Michigan

Berrien County Historical Association
313 North Cass Street
Berrien Springs, Michigan 49103

Printed in the United States of America.
Published by the Berrien County Historical Association.

ISBN 0-9660808-4-X

Cover design by John K. Hopkins
HOPKINS STUDIO, Berrien Springs, Michigan

Table of Contents

Introduction

Greetings from Buchanan, Michigan, the second book in the Berrien County Historical Association's Historic Photobook series, provides an illustrated look at the growth and progress of Buchanan. Buchanan, Michigan, has a long and rich history stretching from its founding on McCoy's Creek. The story of Buchanan begins in 1842 when John Hamilton platted the village and named it Buchanan in honor of United States Senator James Buchanan.

We intended this book to provide a general overview of Buchanan's history with brief narratives illustrated with photographs and postcard images. Whenever possible, we tried to connect individuals or families to places and events. We identified people in photographs as well as possible, given the difficulty in reading old handwriting and the original misidentification of people or places. For these errors, we apologize to those families whose ancestor is misnamed. Readers who inform us of these errors will help us adjust and correct the historical record. Just as we tried to include names and identities, however, this book is not intended to be a comprehensive genealogical listing of the area's families.

Several institutions and individuals made their photographic collections available for *Greetings From Buchanan.* We want to thank the generous folks from the Buchanan District Library whose East Collection of photographs serve as the core collection featured in this book. We also thank the *Berrien County Record* newspaper for providing numerous photographs from its archives; Donald F. Ryman for the use of his private collection; Wayne Wilcox at the Faith United Methodist Church for photographs and church history; and Esther Florey for the use of Dale E. Florey's photograph collection.

We also want to acknowledge the time and effort that Donald F. Ryman and Thomas Kent invested in helping us to read and proof this publication to correct as many errors as possible. Any remaining errors, of course, are ours alone.

We hope you enjoy reading this book as much as we enjoyed bringing it to you.

Leo J. Goodsell
Robert C. Myers
August 2005

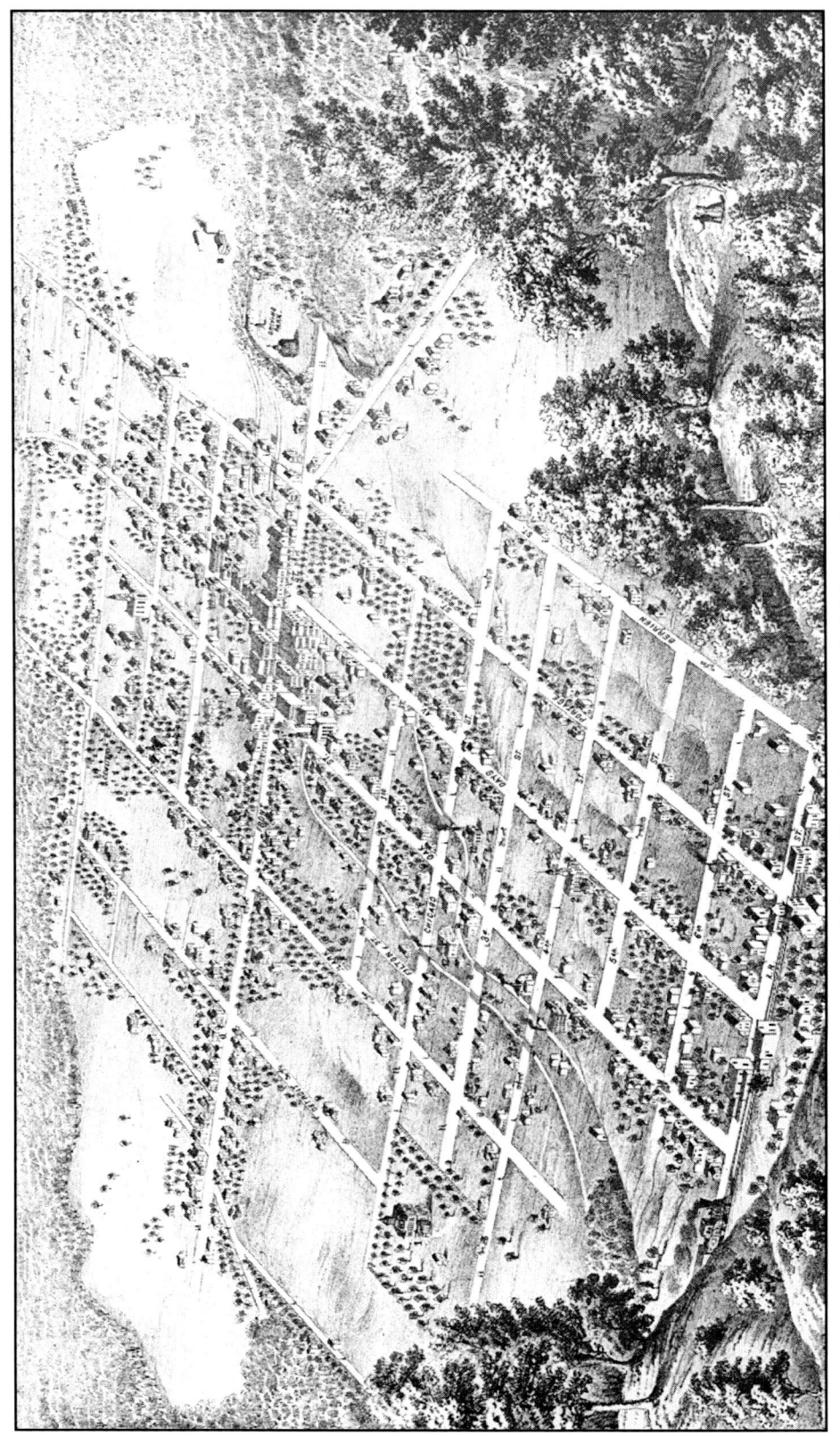

Birdseye View of Buchanan, Michigan, 1873.

Chapter 1
James Buchanan

Buchanan, Michigan, is one of several towns in the Union named for James Buchanan, the fifteenth president of the United States. Besides the city in Berrien County, towns in Georgia, New York, Iowa, Virginia and North Dakota are all named for James Buchanan. In addition, a town in Liberia on the African Continent bears the name Buchanan. In most ratings of presidents in terms of effectiveness in office, however, Buchanan ranks at or near the bottom. Only the corrupt and inept Warren G. Harding edges him out for the dubious distinction of America's poorest chief executive. Buchanan's dismal rating, however, overlooks an outstanding public service career that in many ways belies his low standing with historians. Buchanan took office in 1857 as the slavery issue divided America and the nation headed into civil war. His failure to prevent the war made him a scapegoat, but some historians have noted that Abraham Lincoln (consistently ranked first among presidents) also failed to stave off conflict.

James Buchanan was born near Mercersburg, Pennsylvania, on April 23, 1791, the son of Irish immigrants. He studied law at Dickinson College, was admitted to the bar in 1813, served briefly in the War of 1812, and won election to the Pennsylvania Assembly as a Federalist. Tragedy touched Buchanan's life in 1819. He became engaged to Ann Coleman, daughter of a wealthy ironmaster, but his fiancée's family disapproved of the match and rumors spread that Buchanan was a fortune hunter. Ann broke off the engagement. She died a week later, possibly a suicide. Buchanan never married and became the nation's only bachelor president. A niece, Harriet Lane, served as first lady during his presidency.

Buchanan won election to the U. S. House of Representatives in 1820, and served five consecutive terms, from 1821 to 1831. After the demise of the Federalist party, he shifted his allegiance to Andrew Jackson and the Democrats and helped Jackson in his campaign for the presidency in 1824. Although Jackson won the popular vote, the U. S. House of Representatives decided the election in favor of John Quincy Adams. A bitter Jackson accused Buchanan of conspiring with Adams and Henry Clay to cheat him of his victory. Buchanan denied the charges, but the personal rift between himself and Old Hickory lingered.

A duel over political patronage erupted between Buchanan and George M. Dallas after Jackson won the presidential election of 1828. The fight led Jackson to award Buchanan the appointment of minister to Russia, a post he held from 1832 to 1834. Buchanan negotiated the first commercial treaty between the two nations.

After Buchanan's return from Russia, Pennsylvania's legislature elected him to the United States Senate in 1833. He served two terms in the senate. During that time, he strove to retain a balance between federal power and states' rights. He fended off the attempts of the great Whig senator and orator, Daniel Webster, to expand the federal government, and those of Democratic senator John C. Calhoun to strengthen states' powers.

It was during his first term as senator, not his presidency, that Buchanan loaned his name to the new village of Buchanan and Buchanan Township in Berrien County. In the 1830s, Michigan Territory sought to enter the Union. When conflict arose with Ohio over the states' shared border, the Pennsylvania senator spoke out in favor of Michigan and endeared himself to residents of the Wolverine State. Buchanan supported Michigan, however, largely because he wished to maintain a balance between slave and free states. He realized his goal when Arkansas entered the Union in June 1836 as a slave state, followed by Michigan on January 26, 1837, as a free state. The Michigan Legislature recognized Buchanan's work six weeks later when, on March 11, 1837, it approved an act creating a new township in Berrien County named in his honor. No village then existed in the township, but on July 21, 1842, John Hamilton platted the village of Buchanan, probably naming it in honor of the township.

Although re-elected to the senate in 1845, Buchanan resigned his seat to accept President James K. Polk's offer to serve as U. S. secretary of state. Buchanan oversaw several critical foreign issues, including the Oregon boundary dispute with Great Britain in which he negotiated a compromise treaty and averted a war, and the dispute with Mexico over Texas that led to the Mexican War. After the Polk Administration ended in 1849, Buchanan retired to "Wheatland," his country estate outside Lancaster, Pennsylvania. He campaigned for the Democratic presidential nomination in 1852, but the nod went instead to Franklin Pierce. President Pierce appointed Buchanan U. S. envoy to Great Britain.

As envoy, Buchanan became embroiled in the Ostend Manifesto of 1854. He and other American ministers in Europe met at Ostend, Belgium, to devise ways to persuade Spain to sell Cuba to the United States. Their recommendations included President Pierce's instructions to declare that the United States would take Cuba by force if Spain refused to sell. Buchanan signed the document, which became known as the "Ostend Manifesto," under protest. Reports of the Manifesto raised a furor in America, for Cuba would presumably be admitted to the Union as a new slave state. Opponents wielded the controversy as a political club against the Democrats. President Pierce kept silent and allowed the public to believe that the ministers had drafted the document of their own accord.

Nevertheless, when Buchanan returned to America in 1856 he had amassed considerable political clout. His stay in England had kept him out of the controversy over the Kansas-Nebraska Act of 1854, which repealed the Missouri Compromise and opened the Western territories to slavery. With much help from powerful Southern backers, Buchanan secured the Democratic presidential nomination. He ran in opposition to the candidate of the newly-formed Republican party; antislavery advocate John C. Fremont; and the nominee of the American (Know-Nothing) party, former President Millard Fillmore. Buchanan received fewer popular votes than the combined total of his two opponents, but he won 174 electoral votes and the presidency.

President Buchanan wrote that the foremost object of his administration would be to halt "the agitation of the slavery question at the North" and to "destroy sectional parties." Despite his best efforts, however, the slavery issue overwhelmed his presidency. Buchanan worked diligently to achieve compromises over the slavery issue, but his attempts to walk a political tightrope forced him into paradoxical arguments. In his first term as senator, Buchanan had taken a somewhat ambiguous stance on slavery. He pronounced the "peculiar institution" morally wrong, but maintained that the federal government was obligated to protect slavery where it already existed.

Buchanan had the misfortune to become president just as the simmering slavery issue came to a boil. A natural compromiser, the nation's fifteenth chief executive took office just when no one, North or South, had any inclination to compromise. In 1854, the Kansas-Nebraska Act nullified the Missouri Compromise and opened the West to slavery expansion. Two days before Buchanan's inauguration, the U. S. Supreme Court handed down its decision in the Dred Scott case. The Court held that Dred Scott, a slave, would remain in bondage even though his owner had taken him to Minnesota, a territory from which Congress had barred slavery. Kansas erupted in open warfare between pro- and anti-slavery factions. Radical abolitionist John Brown, whose sons had murdered several pro-slavery men in Kansas, led a raid on the government arsenal at Harper's Ferry in a doomed attempt to arm and lead a slave insurrection. Convicted and hanged for murder and treason, Brown became an anti-slavery martyr.

Through all of this turmoil, Buchanan strove to hold the Union together. His conciliatory stance, however, gained him little credit with either the North or South. In his last annual message to Congress in December 1860, Buchanan blamed the national crisis on abolitionists and the North's continued anti-slavery agitation. South Carolina, however, had already seceded. Other Southern secessionists were determined to follow the Palmetto State's lead, and Northern radicals were just as determined to stop them.

Secession in the South immediately after Abraham Lincoln's election produced a philosophical paralysis in Buchanan. The President declared that states could not legally secede from the Union, but also believed that the federal government could not legally prevent it if they did. In retrospect, however, Buchanan possibly salvaged as much as he could from a hopeless situation. His pro-Southern policies helped keep a lid on secessionist zeal in the border slave states. When he handed the White House over to Abraham Lincoln in March 1861, eight of the fifteen slave states remained in the Union, and four – Missouri, Kentucky, Delaware and Maryland – would stay there.

Buchanan chose not to run for re-election in 1860. The Democratic party had split, the Northern wing nominating Stephen A. Douglas while the Southerners nominated Buchanan's vice president, John C. Breckinridge. Lincoln, the Republican candidate, carried the election. As Buchanan left the White House, he remarked to his successor, "If you are as happy, my dear sir, on entering this house as I am in leaving it and returning home, you are the happiest man in this country."

Buchanan retired to Wheatland, where he spent the war years quietly but loyally supporting the war to restore the Union. He published a book, *Mr. Buchanan's Administration on the Eve of the Rebellion,* in 1866, in defense of his actions as president. He died at his beloved Wheatland in 1868.

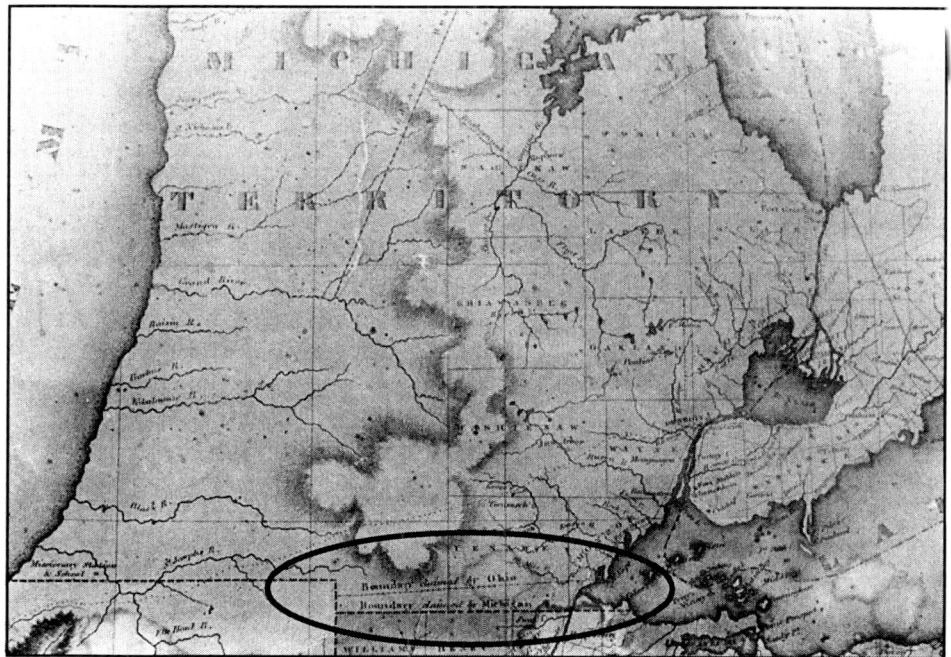

Detail from "Lay's Map of the United States, 1827," showing the disputed "Toledo Strip" highlighted on the Michigan-Ohio border. Gratitude for James Buchanan's work on Michigan's behalf in the Toledo Strip feud led to John Hamilton naming Buchanan, Michigan, in his honor. *(BCHA Collections)*

James Buchanan

Portrait of President James Buchanan. *(BCHA Collections)*

Chapter 2
Early History

Carey Mission

The first Anglo-European settlement in the present-day Buchanan area was a Baptist mission to the Indians called Carey. The mission stood about five miles east of Buchanan. Carey's lofty goals of "civilizing" the area Potawatomi ultimately failed. The mission and school did, however, inadvertantly help open southwest Michigan to white immigration to the area by serving as a location where settlers could establish themselves before acquiring their own land. Several founding residents first came to Carey upon arriving in Berrien County. These men included Squire Thompson, who helped found Niles, and Calvin Britain, who platted the village of St. Joseph.

The Chicago Treaty of 1821 made Carey possible. Before settlers could obtain legal title to land, the United States government first had to buy it from the resident Indian nations. Although Michigan was politically a territory of the United States, the federal government considered the actual land the property of its Indian inhabitants. To obtain that land for settlement, the government needed to acquire it by treaty, just as though the Indian tribes were foreign nations — which, in a legal sense, they were. As with any treaties made with foreign countries, these land cessions were subject to approval by the United States Senate.

The Chicago Treaty of 1821 was the first land cession treaty involving present-day Berrien County. Signed on August 29, 1821, between United States Commissioners Lewis Cass and Solomon Sibley and the Ottawa, Ojibwa and Potawatomi nations, the Treaty of Chicago ceded virtually all of southwest Michigan to the United States. Only the portion of land southwest of the St. Joseph River remained Indian property. Besides other consider-ations, the treaty gave the Ottawa annual cash payments of one thousand dollars in perpe-tuity while the Potawatomi received payments of five thousand dollars per year for twenty years.

The treaty not only left land on the west side of the St. Joseph River in Indian hands, but also appropriated funds for the government's Indian civilization program. Besides cash annuities, the treaty authorized fifteen hundred dollars for "the support of a Blacksmith, of a Teacher and of a person to instruct the Ottawas in agriculture and in the purchase of cattle and farming utensils." The treaty allotted the Potawatomi one thousand dollars per year for the same purpose. One square mile of land on both the Grand and St. Joseph Rivers, within the remaining Indian lands, were to be set aside for establishment of the blacksmith and school.

In dealing with the complex Indian situation, the United States government adopted the "civilization policy." The civilization program was an attempt by the government to persuade the Indians to give up what American officials considered an overdependence on hunting and fishing, which required large land areas. Instead, the civilized Indians would be transformed into the American ideal: land-owning, tax-paying farmers. The Indians would also benefit from government-sponsored educational programs, which would prepare them for eventual assimilation into American society.

Part of the motivation behind the civilization policy was an honest – if naive - humanitarian desire on the part of many government officials to teach the Indians the benefits of American society and educate them so they could enter that society. The policy also expressed the strong feelings of a sizeable portion of the American public that the Indians were being treated shamefully. But while a handful of groups and individuals argued that the Indians should not be compelled to remove westward, the civilization policy never took precedence over the desire to relieve the Indians of their land.

Carey and its founder, Isaac McCoy, played an important role in the Civilization Program. McCoy was born in 1784 in Fayette County, Pennsylvania. He joined the Baptist Church as a boy, and as a young man began preaching as a lay minister. In 1803, he felt called to begin a ministry at Vincennes, in Indiana Territory. Before he set out, McCoy decided to take a wife. On October 6, 1803, he married sixteen year-old Christiana "Kittie" Polke, a relative of the future president of the United States. The couple settled in Vincennes, where McCoy eked out a precarious living as a lay preacher and town jailor. At length he was asked to pastor a small Baptist church at Maria Creek, near Vincennes. The church ordained him on October 13, 1810.

McCoy soon conceived a plan for the formation of "societies for domestick missions." These societies would be composed of associations of Baptist churches, which would raise money to support missionary efforts among settlers on the Western frontier. After some persuasion, the Long Run Association of Baptist churches in Kentucky formed a missionary society and in 1816 asked McCoy to make a tour of southern Illinois and Missouri to determine where preaching points might be established.

The journey proved to be a turning point in McCoy's life. The tour required three months, and everywhere he went McCoy witnessed firsthand the destitute condition of the Indians. In rags, half-starved and inebriated, the Indians' situation was desperate. Their plight haunted him, and when McCoy returned to Vincennes he was resolved to do something to ameliorate their condition.

In 1819, following an extensive preaching tour of southern Indiana and Illinois, McCoy began a school for Indian children on Raccoon Creek near the Wabash River in Indiana. McCoy's work was financed by the Board of Managers of the Board of Foreign Missions of the Baptist church. A year later, McCoy relocated his school in Fort Wayne, Indiana. Despite modest success, McCoy's mission at Fort Wayne was short-lived. American settlers were arriving in ever-increasing numbers, accompanied by the omnipresent whiskey traders. McCoy soon came to realize that the encroaching settlers would swiftly undo whatever progress he made to help the Indians improve their lot.

In the spring of 1821, a St. Joseph River valley chief named Menominee visited McCoy. McCoy and Menominee enjoyed an amiable discussion on religion and American-Indian relations, and the conversation concluded with Menominee inviting McCoy to visit his village. There the Baptist missionary received an enthusiastic welcome from the Potawatomi. This visit, coupled with McCoy's knowledge of the impending Treaty of Chicago, prompted him to consider moving his school and mission to the St. Joseph River region. McCoy knew that the treaty would probably allow the Potawatomi to retain a reservation in the area, and believed that even forty acres would be sufficient to provide a buffer zone between them and the white settlers. McCoy hoped that the Potawatomi would invite him to establish his school on their reservation.

In the winter of 1821-1822, Isaac McCoy traveled to Philadelphia and Washington, D.C., to lay his plans before the Board of Foreign Missions and petition for his appointment as the teacher for the Potawatomi. A prospective missionary named John Sears accompanied him. In Washington, all went to McCoy's satisfaction. His patrons, the Board of Foreign Missions, authorized him to discontinue the Fort Wayne mission and empowered him to select other missionaries and helpers as needed. The board also appropriated five hundred dollars for the construction of a new mission house and approved his request to seek financial aid from the government. McCoy then met with Secretary of War John C. Calhoun. Calhoun readily agreed to McCoy's appointment as teacher for the Potawatomi, and to John Sears as teacher for the Ottawa. He also assented to McCoy's request that the government pay two-thirds of the cost of a mission house.

Upon his return to Fort Wayne, McCoy began preparations for the new St. Joseph River mission. Governor Lewis Cass, who had been appointed Superintendent of Indian Affairs, informed McCoy that the War Department had placed all responsibility for implementing the Treaty of Chicago in his hands, and he was willing to give McCoy all the appointments specified in the treaty. With the recent War of 1812 in mind, Cass noted that it would be a "paramount duty" to secure the Indians' loyalty to the United States and discourage any affection for a foreign power. They must be kept from liquor at all costs. To protect the Indians from traders, McCoy would superintend their spending of annuity payments. McCoy was also required to teach them the concept of land ownership and the benefits of life as law-abiding farmers. The government would pay McCoy an annual salary of $400, and the blacksmith $365. McCoy would also have the superintendency of the Grand River mission.

The location selected for the mission was near the village of Chief Topinabe, about one and one-quarter miles southwest of the St. Joseph River. McCoy named it Carey in honor of William Carey, an English Baptist missionary in Serampore, India. Construction of the mission buildings, beginning with the blacksmith shop, began on October 22. McCoy was assisted by several hired hands who had come along as a work crew. In December, Isaac and Christiana McCoy, their eight children, and eighteen pupils from the Fort Wayne mission made a one hundred-mile trek through deep snow to the site of their new home.

Construction of the buildings at Carey progressed rapidly. By the end of December the little establishment included an apartment house, kitchen, smith shop and meat house, although none of them were completely finished. The Potawatomi stopped by frequently, mostly in hopes that the blacksmith shop would be in operation and they could have muskets and tools repaired. On New Year's Day, 1823, Potawatomi leaders Topinabe and Chebass, and about forty other Potawatomi men, women and children came to Carey to wish McCoy and the other arrivals a happy New Year. The festivities, learned from French traders, involved much handshaking and kissing, although McCoy persuaded them to forego the latter.

The Carey school opened on Monday, January 27, 1823, with twenty-nine Indian students. Still half-finished, the school house was without a floor or chimney, and was filled with smoke from its only source of heat: a large fire in the center of the room. All of the students were fed, clothed and housed at McCoy's expense, and the Indian children had voracious appetites. In mid-winter, far from civilization, food was difficult to come by. An expected shipment of flour failed to appear, and by February 1 the supply of corn was gone. Some of the boys walked five miles to borrow a barrel of flour and a bushel of corn from a French trader, but in a week that too was gone.

In desperation, McCoy set off on foot through the snow, hoping to purchase some corn from the Indians. He chanced to meet French trader Joseph Bertrand, to whom he explained his plight. The old Frenchman listened to McCoy's story, then explained that the Indians had scattered to their hunting camps. They would be almost impossible to find, and would probably have no corn to spare anyway. "But," said Bertrand in broken English, "I got some corn, some flour; I give you half. Suppose you die, I die too." With gifts of food from Bertrand and a few Indians, the people at Carey survived until several wagons filled with flour arrived a few days later.

In late February, Johnston Lykins, who had taught occasionally at Fort Wayne, arrived at Carey. McCoy wrote to Lewis Cass and suggested that the young man be appointed in the place of Sears as the teacher at the Ottawa mission. Cass agreed, and in May 1823 McCoy set off for the Grand River to establish the mission site.

McCoy found the Ottawas distrustful. They were unhappy with the Treaty of Chicago and maintained that they had never authorized their leaders to sell their land. Many were certain that McCoy's real purpose in coming was not to build a school and blacksmith shop but to force them to accede to the treaty terms. But worse than their animosity was the sight of entire bands of Ottawas drunk with whiskey, and wagon loads of the liquor being carried from place to place.

On June 4, as he plodded along on horseback toward Carey, McCoy was deeply discouraged. Deep in thought, he was suddenly struck by an idea that came to him almost as a supernatural revelation. Despite the tremendous labor and expense in building Indian schools, all of the missionary's work was being undone by the whiskey traders. In the end, McCoy realized, "if we remain here, it will be only to witness the decline and ultimate ruin of the people of our charge, for no band of Indians has ever thriven when crowded by white population."

The solution, he decided, was to remove the Indians to the West, beyond the Mississippi River. There they would be free of the white man's corrupting influence. Assisted by missionaries, the Indians would learn farming and mechanical arts, develop their own civil community and eventually become United States citizens. The concept of Indian removal, coupled with civilization efforts, became the driving force of McCoy's life. He immediately wrote letters to congressmen, outlining the concept and pushing for its adoption. In late 1823 he made a trip to Washington, where he presented his removal plans to President James Monroe's administration.

But although McCoy was already planning for its eventual closing, work at Carey was progressing well. In October 1824, Judge John L. Leib, a government commissioner inspecting missions for Governor Cass, reported that Carey had an enrollment of sixty-two Indian students ranging from three to twenty years of age. Most were Potawatomi, with a smattering of Ottawa, Mohegan and a single Miami.

Besides Isaac and Kittie McCoy, the school's staff included the blacksmith and two male and one female teacher. Six other men helped with the farming operations. The children learned English, spelling, reading, writing and arithmetic. Besides their academic classes, the Indian pupils learned the skills required for their successful "civilization" and induction into American society: the boys learned farming or blacksmithing, while the girls practiced sewing, spinning, knitting and weaving.

Life at Carey resembled nothing so much as a military training camp, or perhaps a monastery. A trumpet call woke the students at sunrise, followed soon after by a bell which called them to morning prayers. Chores came next, then breakfast. Classes began at eight o'clock in the morning and continued until noon; lunch was served at half past twelve and the remainder of the day spent in farming or textile production. Shortly after sunset everyone came together for evening prayers, usually accompanied by singing and scripture reading. Saturdays were holidays. Children played and went swimming in the river. Sundays were spent largely in church services, one in the morning and one in the afternoon.

The mission itself included six dwelling houses, a kitchen, a dining room, the schoolhouse and the blacksmith shop, plus nine outbuildings. All were squared timber, chinked with clay, and set on a rectangular plot of ground 330 feet long by 165 feet wide. Although Carey had only been operating for less than two years, McCoy's staff and students had cleared and fenced a field of fifty acres. Most of it was planted in Indian corn, with five acres in oats and one in potatoes. Several smaller fields, totalling twenty-two acres, produced peas, turnips, cabbages, beets and other garden vegetables for the mission dinner tables. An eighteen acre field was set aside as pasture for the eight horses, eight oxen, eighty-eight cattle and fifty-nine sheep kept on the farm. Fifty-nine hogs were being fattened for conversion into ham and sausages.

But despite Judge Leib's glowing appraisal, McCoy was able to view the situation with a more critical eye. Near Carey, he saw "children gathering weeds to boil and eat. I have seen the mother in a swamp, digging roots for her half-starved children. I have seen them feed on animals that had died of disease and had lain until their flesh had become putride." Ironically, Carey's success attracted a growing number of settlers and other, less savory, characters. One of these was Squire Thompson, a Hoosier who came to stay at the mission for a short time and then, to McCoy's dismay, set up a whiskey shop two miles away on the opposite side of the river. Among Thompson's customers were some of the Carey students. McCoy reported that Thompson "is, without doubt, the most troublesome man, and the most flagitious in his conduct in selling liquor to the Indians, of any one I have ever found in the Indian Country." One of the whiskey traders' victims was Topinabe, the elderly and much esteemed Potawatomi *wkama* who had succored Joseph Bertrand during the War of 1812. Topinabe died two days after a fall from his horse while drunk from whiskey.

But Carey, in the meantime, continued to flourish. By August 1826, when Judge Leib returned to Carey for another inspection, the mission boasted an enrollment of seventy-two students — forty-two boys and twenty-eight girls. Moreover, eight alumni had transferred to academies in New York and New Jersey. Leib reported that the farm included 203 fenced acres, on which the students raised fields of wheat and corn, and tended gardens of vegetable produce. A large new storehouse had been added to the settlement. Even more important was a horse-powered gristmill, which enabled the students to grind their own meal. The girls were busy with weaving and spinning, and during the course of the preceding year had woven 185 yards of cloth.

But by this time it was apparent even to an incurable optimist like Leib that the progress at Carey was mostly superficial. While at Carey, the Judge was deeply moved by an eloquent speech delivered by an elderly *wkama*. The Indian told Leib that white men brought whiskey to the Indians and, although the latter were fully aware of its disastrous effects, they were powerless to resist its temptation. Then, drawing himself up proudly, the *wkama* declared "if our great father feels such an interest to preserve us, as you mention, all powerful as he is, why does he not command his people to abstain from seeking in the ways you mention, our destruction. He has but to will it and his will will be done. He can punish. He can save us from the ruin which surrounds us — we can do nothing of ourselves — if whiskey was not brought to us, we should soon cease to think of it, and we should be happier and healthier."

Leib could find no apology for his country. He also noted the rapidly growing number of settlers who were arriving in Berrien County. These people were even then building homes and farms on the land, despite the fact that they had no legal right to claim it. Leib observed that they "to be sure are what are called squatters, but they have penetrated these distant regions with their numerous offspring in search of a healthful clime, and here they have found it, and hope whenever the lands are to be sold that the right of preemption will be granted to them. . . ." The squatters raised a growing chorus of demands for Indian land to be acquired and sold, hoping that the government would then recognize their claims.

Despite McCoy's growing apprehensions about the prospects for successful Indian civilization in Michigan, he was unable to ignore his obligation to establish the long-delayed mission among the Ottawas. In November 1826, he and his family travelled to a site on the Grand River, forty miles from Lake Michigan, where they founded the mission promised in the Treaty of Chicago. McCoy christened the new establishment Thomas, honoring John Thomas, a British medical missionary in India. McCoy turned Thomas over to two subordinates and returned to Carey.

Although he had two Indian missions in Michigan Territory under his supervision, Isaac McCoy continued to lobby Congress in favor of Indian removal. McCoy felt that he was in a race with time, desperately hoping to have the Indians removed from the region before they were utterly destroyed. For their part, most Indians were only lukewarm toward the idea of removal. McCoy was certain that their reluctance was due to the whiskey traders' influence, who feared a loss of their livelihood if the Indians departed. The squatters seemed to be in league with the whiskey traders, taking the view that a drunken Indian would soon be a dead Indian, and a dead Indian would have no need for his land.

By 1828, McCoy's plans for Indian colonization had fully matured. The Baptist missionary conceived a vast area for Indian colonization that would forever separate the Indians from the pernicious effects of the white man. The region for Indian relocation would be bounded on the west by the Rocky Mountains, on the south by Mexican territory, and on the east by the Mississippi River, the state of Missouri, and Arkansas Territory. Land in this Indian Canaan would be set aside for each tribe. There, under the benevolent authority of United States government commissioners, the work of education and civilization begun at Carey could continue. Best of all, Indian removal would be a permanent solution. A large tract of seemingly uninhabitable land east of the Indian country would provide a *cordon sanitare* to separate the Indians from whiskey traders and other corrupting influence.

In June 1828, McCoy received a government commission to explore west of the Mississippi to locate land suitable for Indian colonization. Accompanied by six Indians, McCoy travelled from Carey to St. Louis, Missouri, then set off on a journey that took him about 140 miles into Kansas. He returned convinced that the land would support an Indian population if it were properly used, although his Indian companions were less sanguine. On another expedition that October, McCoy and a larger party of Indians, accompanied by a surgeon, interpreters and two topographers, made a detailed survey map of the region.

McCoy returned from this endeavor with his relocation plans essentially complete. Convinced that there was not a moment to lose, he decided not to stop at Carey but instead went directly to Washington to lobby for Indian removal. McCoy left Johnston Lykins in charge of Carey during his absence. As one of his first duties, Lykins made arrangements for treaty negotiations held at Carey between the Potawatomi and United States Commissioners Lewis Cass and Pierre Menard. The two commissioners signed the Carey Mission Treaty with the Potawatomi on September 20, 1828. Along with other property in Indiana, the Potawatomi surrendered almost all of their remaining lands in present-day Berrien County. Only a small tract of land around Carey itself remained in Indian hands. In return, the Potawatomis received a permanent annuity of $2,000, an additional annuity of $1,000 for a term of twenty years; $30,000 in goods; and an additional $5,000 in cash and $10,000 in goods in 1829. The treaty included another $7,500 for the "civilization" program: clearing and fencing land, and buying farming utensils and domestic animals and a further $1,000 annuity for education. As usual, it also set off certain tracts of land for various individuals.

Isaac McCoy, in the meantime, was in Washington during the transitional period between the administrations of Presidents John Quincy Adams and Andrew Jackson. McCoy found in Andrew Jackson a powerful advocate of Indian removal. From personal experience as an army officer and territorial governor of Florida, Old Hickory had found the absurd whole treaty-making process and its attendant governmental obligations. Jackson entertained a grand vision of American destiny, with Americans from every state and territory expanding across the continent to form a unified nation. Although a staunch supporter of states rights, Jackson saw it as the federal government's duty to remove any impediments to national security and the expansion of America. The Indians constituted such an impediment. McCoy's plans for Indian removal dovetailed with Jackson's expansionist views.

Carey was soon abandoned. When Christiana learned that Isaac had gone directly to Washington, she moved her family to Lexington, Kentucky. Johnston Lykins accompanied her, leaving Carey under the supervision of Robert Simerwell. Isaac McCoy visited Carey for the last time in June 1829 to encourage the Potawatomi to remove from Michigan Territory. His designs were frustrated by a trader who sent over several barrels of cider which McCoy naively distributed. The cider was heavily laced with whiskey, and McCoy's arguments were largely wasted on his inebriated listeners.

McCoy moved his family to Fayette, Missouri, and after another exploration trip into the Kansas River valley returned to Washington to begin a seven months' campaign for

Indian removal. On May 28, 1830, McCoy saw his years of lobbying bear fruit when President Jackson signed the Removal Act of 1830 into law. The legislation provided Jackson with the necessary congressional sanction to carry out his removal policy. The act authorized the president to exchange unorganized public land in the West for Indian-held land in the East. Indians would receive permanent title to the western lands and be paid for any improvements they had made on the lands they surrendered. Congress appropriated $500,000 to fund removal treaty and land session negotiations.

Carey finally closed forever in late 1830 as McCoy prepared to take up the task of Indian civilization in the newly created western Indian territories. As the decade of the 1820s drew to a close, all of the land in Berrien County except that set aside by the Carey Mission Treaty of 1828 had become public land, owned by the United States government. In a few years that too would be gone, ceded by the Potawatomi as they succumbed to pressure to remove to Isaac McCoy's Indian Canaan in Kansas.

When the Indians removed to the West, Isaac McCoy went with them, laboring to the end of his life in a futile effort to create the Indian utopia he had envisioned for so many years. He lived to see most of his plans destroyed as the relentless tide of white emigration flowed into his cherished Indian reservations. He died in Louisville, Kentucky on June 21, 1846.

The Founding of Buchanan

The city of Buchanan originated in 1842, when John Hamilton, a millwright, had the village platted and named it "Buchanan." The town owes its founding to its development as an industrial site. Whereas some towns, like Berrien Springs, started out as market towns and others, like Niles, began as transportation centers, Buchanan owes its existence to milling and manufacturing.

John Hamilton had immigrated to Michigan from his native Virginia in the 1830s and set up a mill operation near Niles on the Dowagiac River. He evidently visited the future site of Buchanan and noted the waterpower potential of McCoy's Creek, for in 1839 he moved there and with Andrew C. Day built a gristmill. Hamilton's partner had come to the area from Delaware County, New York, in 1836. Like Hamilton, Day had considerable experience with mills. He had owned a gristmill in Delaware County and also operated a sawmill there. The two men may have become familiar with McCoy's Creek through Russell McCoy, who with Hiram Wray had built a sawmill at the creek's mouth in 1836.

Russell McCoy, like many of Berrien County's earliest American settlers, had moved to the area to work at the Carey Mission. McCoy's tenure at Carey proved short-lived. The missionaries twice dismissed him from their employ: once for stopping to talk with some girls after kindling the morning fires, and again for swearing at some obstreperous hogs that had broken out of their pen. Carey was closing anyway, the mission staff moving west with the displaced Potawatomi, so McCoy found work for a few years as a boatman on the St. Joseph River. In 1834, he staked a claim on land on McCoy's Creek for his sawmill. Charles Cowles built a shingle mill nearby at the same time, and these two mills had doubtless attracted the experienced eye of John Hamilton.

Hamilton's original plat of the village of Buchanan lay in the extreme southeast corner of section 26 of Buchanan Township. The town would later sprawl out into sections 25, 35 and 36. The township itself had originated with an act of the Michigan Legislature, approved on March 11, 1837, which set off the new township, named it Buchanan, and specified that the first township meeting be held at the home of Charles C. Wallin. A settlement had apparently already started on the town site prior to Hamilton's surveying of streets and lots. When Lorenzo P. Alexander arrived there from his native New York in October of 1841, he found four cabins and a gristmill, sawmill and distillery already in operation.

John Hamilton registered the plat of his new town on July 21, 1842. He apparently had no great ambitions for Buchanan. He had the surveyor plat only forty-four lots in the entire village and gave the new town but three streets, named (rather unimaginatively) Main Street (running north-south) and Front, Second and Third streets (running east-west). The village grew rapidly despite Hamilton's modest plans and settlers soon demanded more lots than Buchanan had to offer. Developers platted new additions to the original village in rapid succession. Albert B. Staples' Addition (1844) and Joseph DeMont's Addition (1845) were followed by two more additions in the 1850s and another six in the 1860s. John Hamilton never lived to see his town grow. He died in Buchanan on August 21, 1846, just four years after he founded the village.

Buchanan's fast growth continued through the mid-nineteenth century, spurred in large part by the arrival of the Michigan Central Railroad in 1849. Buchanan incorporated as a village in 1858, only sixteen years after its founding. Some 860 people already lived in the village at that time, a population that would swell to 1,702 in 1870 and 2,070 in 1884. The town boasted a three-story brick block (retail space on the first floor, offices and/or apartments on the upper floors) by 1860, an achievement bested in Berrien County only in Niles.

By 1870, Buchananites believed with some justification that they resided in one of the finest towns in the American West. A fire on October 31, 1862, destroyed two dozen buildings, including much of the downtown, but residents soon rebuilt. Shade trees lined the streets and they could count six miles of sidewalks. Fine homes and stores had sprung up throughout the village, and residents enjoyed all the amenities of much larger towns, including a tailor shop, dressmakers' shops, a milliner, bakery, photographer's studio and two hotels. That hallmark of civilization, a newspaper (the *Buchanan Vindicator*) had begun publishing in 1858. The *Vindicator* became the *Buchanan Weekly Union* and in 1867 changed its name to become the *Berrien County Record*. That paper remains in existence to the present day as the town's oldest business. Buchanan residents declared proudly that their village had, per capita, more churches and fewer saloons than any town in the county.

As Buchanan celebrated the United States centennial in 1876, its citizens had ample cause for confidence in the future. Already well established, the village had all the requisites for growth. Railroad, river and road systems all converged there to give the town an outstanding transportation network and access to outside markets, McCoy's Creek furnished ample power, and the surrounding farms and forests produced crops, livestock and lumber. The future years would bear out that confident outlook. The village incorporated as the city of Buchanan in 1929. It became the fifth incorporated city in Berrien County, following Niles (1859), Benton Harbor and St. Joseph (1891) and Watervliet (1925).

The Paper Village of Benton

The city of Buchanan was not the first town platted in present-day Buchanan Township. That honor fell instead to the village of Benton.

The St. Joseph River and Great Sauk Trail (later the Chicago Road) offered natural advantages to the creation of a village. Michigan's early settlers platted numerous villages in Berrien County. Some of these owed their founding to natural advantages — St. Joseph and New Buffalo at the mouths of rivers, and Buchanan where McCoy's Creek furnished ample waterpower for mills. Others, like the village of Benton, came about as purely speculative ventures. Benton had no relationship to Benton Harbor, a village founded much later, and even preceded the township of Benton. The village of Benton was located in Section 25 of Buchanan Township, immediately across the river from the present-day city of Buchanan.

Two settlers of Buchanan Township, William Broadhurst and Joseph Stephens, founded Benton in 1832. Broadhurst had purchased the land that June at a United States government land office, and that summer he and Stephens hired a civil engineer named John Woolman to survey and plat a village on the property. On August 18, 1832, the two men registered their new town with the Berrien County register of deeds. They named it Benton in honor of Thomas Hart Benton, a prominent United States senator from Missouri.

The concept of a speculative town like Benton worked this way: the town proprietors would purchase a likely-looking tract of land, which at the government land office could be had for as little as $1.25 an acre. They would then have the town platted — laid out into streets and lots by a surveyor. If the town "took" - that is, if people could be induced to settle there - the lots would skyrocket in value. The speculators might sell the land that they had purchased at $1.25 an acre for $10 to $50 dollars a lot, or even more.

Broadhurst and Stephens had the surveyor lay out seven streets in Benton: Water, Front and Second streets ran north-south, with Water Street naturally running along the St. Joseph River. Mulberry, Main, Cherry and Sugar Streets ran east-west. Benton contained 106 lots; the plat specified that the proprietors donated lot 36 to the public on which to build a church, and lot 97 for a school. Broadhurst and Stephens intended their largess to be an added inducement for people to settle in Benton.

But Benton remained a town in name only. The intended attraction for settlers may have been the newly emerging riverboat traffic, but in this the town proved unsuccessful. People settled instead in the rapidly growing villages of Niles and Bertrand, or just across the river along McCoy's Creek where Buchanan would be platted in 1842. Settlers soon forgot about the village of Benton. No one ever built there and the property remained farmland. Today, a residential area covers the site of Benton, leaving no trace of the town platted by William Broadhurst and Joseph Stephens.

Winter scene on McCoy's Creek. The creek's excellent waterpower potential led to the founding and development of Buchanan as an industrial village. *(Courtesy Buchanan District Library)*

The Moccasin Bluff area north of Buchanan. Moccasin Bluff ranks among the most important of Michigan's Native American archaeological sites. Added to the National Register of Historic Places in 1977. Archaeologists from the University of Michigan explored the site in 1948 and determined that Native Americans occupation began there no later than about 8500 B.C. Anglo-American settlers in the 1830s named the site for a Potawatomi leader named Kawk-Moc-a-sin whose village of about three hundred people stood nearby. *(Courtesy Buchanan District Library)*

Cut through Moccasin Bluff, ca. 1900. Construction of the St. Joseph Valley Railroad in 1880 and, later, Red Bud Trail destroyed some of the archaeological site. The Riverside Mobile Home Court occupies a large portion of the site, with private residences on other parts. *(Courtesy Buchanan District Library)*

The road along Moccasin Bluff eventually became Red Bud Trail, named for the beautiful redbud trees that line the route. The red bud, *Cercis canadensis,* ranges from Connecticut to southern Wisconsin and as far south as Texas and Florida. *(Courtesy Buchanan District Library)*

Winter scene at Moccasin Bluff. The bluff is part of the Valparaiso Moraine, and consists of glacial rock and soil debris. *(Courtesy Buchanan District Library)*

Two visitors enjoy a drink of fresh cold water at Moccasin Bluff, ca. 1905. *(Courtesy Buchanan District Library)*

Chamberlain Hills on the south side of Buchanan. This area of high ground was named for its owner, Benjamin Chamberlain, who farmed nearly 150 acres there during the 1870s-1910s. *(Courtesy Buchanan District Library)*

Looking north over Buchanan, ca. 1920. The Michigan Central Railroad tracks are in the foreground. *(Dale E. Florey Collection)*

A. H. Bunker took up residence on the site of the paper village of Benton prior to 1860, where he evidently built this log cabin. *(Courtesy Buchanan District Library)*

The St. Joseph River near Buchanan. The river served as an important commercial highway from Lake Michigan into southwest Michigan and northern Indiana. Steamboats began running from St. Joseph to South Bend as early as 1831. The area's colonial French settlers at first called it the River of the Miamis for the Miami Indians who lived in the region. By the mid-18th century they had taken to calling it the River St. Joseph, honoring the patron saint of New France. *(Courtesy Buchanan District Library)*

Batchelor's Island, in the 1870s, consisted of a large island in the St. Joseph River about two miles downstream from Buchanan. It got its name not as a refuge for unmarried men but from its owner, Asa W. Batchelor. *(Courtesy Buchanan District Library)*

Spectacular summer scenery along the St. Joseph River attracted tourists to the Berrien County area. Many resorts and campgrounds sprang up in the area to cater to the visitors tried to escape the heat of the big cities. *(Courtesy Berrien County Record)*

Berrien County's early settlers built sawmills and gristmills wherever they found a stream that furnished sufficient waterpower. Most of Buchanan's mills had steam engines as auxiliary power sources for dry spells. *(Courtesy Buchanan District Library)*

Andrew C. Day, shown here with his wife, Betsy, was one of Buchanan's founders. He came to Berrien County from New York in 1836, and with John Hamilton built a gristmill on the future site of the Buchanan in 1839. He later served as president of the Buchanan Manufacturing Company. He resided in Buchanan until his death on November 10, 1885. *(Courtesy Buchanan District Library)*

Mahala Gates Mansfield was born in New York State in 1812. In the spring of 1842, she and her husband, Ira, sold their farm and tavern and set off overland for Crystal Lake, Illinois, forty-two miles northwest of Chicago. The party included the Mansfield's four children and Ira's grandmother, niece and three brothers. When they arrived in Crystal Lake, relatives already living there showed Ira some farm acreage. Ira, disgusted with the "black muck" soil, declared that he would not accept the land if someone gave it to him, and headed back to New York. The family ran out of money when they reached Bertrand. Fortunately, they happened upon Jacob D. Dutton, who owned a saw-mill and vacant log cabin on McCoy's Creek. Dutton offered Ira lodging and employment. Thus the Mansfields, almost by chance, settled in Buchanan on the Fourth of July 1842 and lived there the rest of their lives. Mahala, who outlived her husband, died in Buchanan on October 24, 1883. *(Courtesy Buchanan District Library)*

Chapter 3
Agriculture

Buchanan offered many advantages to farmers. Fertile soil and a favorable climate with temperatures moderated by Lake Michigan made for good growing conditions. The numerous mills that sprang up along McCoy's Creek in the village proper allowed farmers to grind their grain into flour for easy shipment to market. In many parts of America, poor roads and a lack of rail and water transportation made shipment of farm produce prohibitively expensive, but Buchanan's farmers could send produce, meat and wool to market at relatively low cost. The St. Joseph River provided access to South Bend, Indiana, and the port of St. Joseph, while the Michigan Central Railroad tied the Buchanan farms to Chicago and Detroit. Buchanan's soil, climate and transportation advantages made its farms some of the most prosperous in the region.

Concentrating grain into liquid – whisky – made shipping even cheaper. Julius Russell opened a distillery in Buchanan in 1840, joining others already operating in Berrien Springs and St. Joseph. Whisky always enjoyed a ready market among thirsty Americans. General stores usually had a keg of whisky in a back room where, after shopping, the customer could help himself to what was known as a "treat." A hefty slug of whisky deadened the fatigue caused by backbreaking farm labor, and in some parts of America a man's neighbors considered him a moderate drinker if he consumed less than a quart of whisky a day. Farmers often considered whisky essential for barn-raisings and other community endeavors. In nearby Niles Township in 1830, for example, residents had nearly completed the construction of the area's first flour mill but refused to place the last bents without a jug of whisky. They dispatched Obed P. Lacey, a teetotaler, for the necessary jug. When Lacey returned he hid the jug in some nearby bushes and arrived at the worksite without it. General dissatisfaction ensued and several workers left in disgust. Lacey was eventually induced to retrieve the jug and as participants later recalled, "under its exhilarating influence, the last bents went up with a will."

The federal government had recognized that legal title to the land belonged to its Potawatomi inhabitants, and in the 1820s and 1830s agents set out to acquire that land through treaties. By dint of persuasion and coercion, the Potawatomi ceded land in Berrien County that lay east and north of the St. Joseph River in the Chicago Treaty of 1821 and most of the land south and west of the river in the Carey Mission Treaty of 1828 Those treaties left the Potawatomi a small tract of land in the Buchanan area, but title to even that was extinguished in the Chicago Treaty of 1833. After that, the land belonged to the federal government, which proceeded to sell it off to land-hungry farmers and speculators.

Some of Buchanan's earliest residents occupied the land without purchasing it – "squatters," in the parlance of the day. Most settlers, however, bought the land properly at a government land office. Berrien County, as part of Michigan, had once been part of the Northwest Territory. The Northwest Territory, made up of lands northwest of the Ohio River and east of the Mississippi, included the present-day states of Michigan, Ohio, Indiana, Illinois, and Wisconsin. But when the United States acquired the Northwest Territory from England after the American Revolution, no one had decided exactly how the lands were going to be sold to prospective settlers. Some congressmen had advocated the Southern system of land sales, a method that involved a buyer obtaining a warrant, selecting the tract of land he wanted and then having it surveyed. Other congressmen, however, favored the New England system, in which the land was surveyed prior to its sale. The Land Ordinance of 1785 finally decided the question in favor of the New England system. According to the New England system, surveyors laid out the land belonging to the federal government into townships six miles square, each one comprised of thirty-six sections one mile square. Each section, then, contained 640 acres. Surveyors could then divide the sections into half sections, quarter sections, or even eighth sections. An eighth section, or eighty acres, could produce enough crops to sustain a family.

Surveying with what was termed the "rectangular" method necessitated the creation of a Base Line and Principal Meridian: imaginary lines running east-west and north-south. The Base Line in Michigan ran straight west from a point on Lake St. Clair to Lake Michigan, while the Principal Meridian ran due north from the Michigan-Ohio border, dividing the counties of Lenawee and Hillsdale. North-south rows of townships were referred to as ranges, and were described as being either east or west of the Principal Meridian; horizontal rows of townships were referred to as being either north or south of the Base Line. Buchanan Township is Town 7 South, Range 18 West; in other words, seven townships south of the Base Line and eighteen townships west of the Principle Meridian.

Land surveys of Michigan Territory were carried out under orders of the U.S. War Department, the actual work being conducted by the United States Topographical Engineers assisted by a corps of civil engineers. The surveyor, accompanied by two chainmen and an axeman, had the task of running an exactly straight line in a given direction. The chainmen measured the line in increments of one mile, and the axemen cleared the line of brush and marked the corners with a stake. The surveyor also kept detailed notes of the characteristics of the soil and trees he encountered in each section, along with remarks about rivers, streams or any unusual topographical features.

As it worked out, Berrien County's meandering Lake Michigan shoreline and the natural division of the St. Joseph River prevented its survey into the neat, square, thirty-six section townships. Some townships wound up with a few extra sections, while others had a few less than the regulation thirty-six, so as to fit within the natural borders. In the original platting of the county Buchanan Township lost several sections on its east side because the St. Joseph River originally served as the boundary between it and Niles Township. The sections east of the river that rightfully belonged to Buchanan went to Niles instead. In 1891, the Michigan Legislature rectified that injustice and bestowed upon Buchanan Township the missing sections of land east of the river so that it, too, had its proper thirty-six sections.

As the surveyors completed their work, the federal government established land offices to allow settlers to purchase government lands. The first of these was established in Detroit in 1816, with subsequent land offices opening in Monroe in 1823, White Pigeon in 1831, Kalamazoo in 1834, and Flint and Ionia in 1836. Most of Buchanan's early farmers bought their land in either Kalamazoo or White Pigeon. Congress lowered the minimum price for public lands to $1.25 an acre by 1820, and also reduced the minimum acreage that could be purchased to eighty acres. A settler could, therefore, buy an eighty-acre farm in Michigan for only one hundred dollars.

A history of Berrien County published in 1880 remarked that Buchanan Township featured an undulating topography. The rolling hills were not so steep, however, as to preclude clearing the land for fields, and Moccasin Bluff on the north side of the village represented the highest elevation in the vicinity. The same source noted that the clay loam and sand soil "is very rich and productive, and particularly adapted to the growth of cereals." Hardwood trees covered most of the area. Early settlers in the 1830s and 1840s busied themselves in hacking down the forests and planting crops.

As the settlers created farm fields and millponds, they inadvertently established ideal breeding grounds for mosquitoes that carried the parasite that caused a form of malaria called ague. An ague attack began with chills and violent shaking. Severe fever and backache followed the chills, and finally the victims endured profuse sweating until the attack was over. Although rarely fatal, ague attacks left victims wan and debilitated.

Recalling an ague attack, one person wrote "You felt as though you had gone through some kind of collision, thrashing-machine or jarring-machine, and came out not killed, but next thing to it. You felt weak, an though you had run too far after something and then didn't catch it."

The disease was a severe problem, but pioneer settlers were nothing if not resourceful. One pragmatic Buchanan woman saw no reason for her husband to lie idle while suffering through an attack, so she rigged up a harness and fastened it to him Whenever her husband shook with ague chills, she hooked his harness to either the baby cradle or butter churn and used his motion to rock the baby or churn the butter.

The medical world had fortunately arrived at a remedy for ague, although nothing then available in the physicians' medical arsenal could cure it. Quinine, a drug that interfered with the growth and reproduction of the parasite in the bloodstream that caused ague, became available in purified form in the 1820s. Quinine was common in almost every Michigan household. Some men even carried the bitter substance along in their vest pockets so they could have a pinch while at work. By the late 19th century, better land drainage had helped reduce the incidence of ague.

Ague or no, farmers took full advantage of Buchanan's arable soil. The 1874 agricultural census reported that Buchanan Township contained 15,613 acres of farmland and 179 farmhouses. These farms produced 28,481 bushels of wheat, 44,999 bushels of corn, 12,707 bushels of other grains, 6,896 bushels of apples, 1,040 bushels of peaches and 300 bushels of pears.

During the late 19th and early 20th centuries, Buchanan's economy shifted from agriculture and farm-related industries (such as flour mills) toward industrial production. Agriculture continued to dominate the economy of the surrounding township, however, and remains an important part of Buchanan's economic and social fabric.

Rare quadruplet lambs born on the Austin C. Sarver farm on February 15, 1937. Ewes typically give birth to one lamb and sometimes two, but four was unusual indeed. Austin and Katherine Sarver farmed in Bertrand Township near Dayton. *(Courtesy Buchanan District Library)*

A large family group at the Eli Mitchell farm, ca.1900. Big families meant extra hands to help during the labor-intensive planting and harvest seasons. *(Courtesy Buchanan District Library)*

Wagon and team on the Pears farm. *(Courtesy Buchanan District Library)*

Picnic at the Eli Mitchell home. Eli and Mary Mitchell farmed a large area around Madron Lake. *(Courtesy Buchanan District Library)*

An unidentified farmhouse. *(Courtesy Buchanan District Library)*

Benjamin Tomlinson at the controls of a steam traction engine, ca. 1905. The steam engines' spinning flywheel and leather belt powered all sorts of farm equipment: threshing
machines, sawmills and buzz saws. Few farmers owned the expensive steam engines
themselves – instead, the engine and its owner traveled from farm to farm at harvest time.
(Courtesy Buchanan District Library)

Ginsing beds. The root of the ginseng herb has long been popular for its medical qualities.
(Courtesy Buchanan District Library)

Berry pickers at the Andrew Huss farm, ca. 1910. Andrew and Clara Huss rar. a thirty-acre farm a mile northeast of Buchanan. *(Courtesy Buchanan District Library)*

Spafford's Fox farm. *(Courtesy Buchanan District Library)*

The Eli and Mary Mitchell family posed outside their fashionable farmhouse, ca. 1900. The windmill to the right of the house harnessed the wind to pump water for the household as well as the farm livestock. *(Courtesy Buchanan District Library)*

A family portrait at the "Eastman farm," ca. 1905. A boy and one of the women appear with firearms at the ready. The location is probably at the W. W. Eastman farm in Bertrand Township, about three miles southwest of Buchanan. *(Courtesy Buchanan District Library)*

The farmhouse of Milton J. and Julia M. (Feather) Bliss, ca. 1910. The Bliss family farmed 124 acres east of Buchanan in Niles Township. *(Courtesy Buchanan District Library)*

The farm of William Broceus. William Broceus farmed 103.5 acres on present-day Red Bud Trail about three miles north of Buchanan. *(Courtesy Buchanan District Library)*

William and Phoebe Broceus.
(Courtesy Buchanan District Library)

Homer George Hathaway aboard the farm's most humble vehicle: a manure spreader. Farm cattle had the added benefit of creating natural fertilizer for the fields. Hathaway later worked as a drill grinder for Clark Equipment Company. He died in 1925 at age 59. *(Courtesy Buchanan District Library)*

The Pears Grain Company in the old skating rink. *(Courtesy Buchanan District Library)*

The William Broceus farmhouse, ca. 1900. A native Michigander, Broceus and his wife Phoebe farmed the land until his death in 1906. *(Courtesy Buchanan District Library)*

Threshing day on a Buchanan area farm. Note the huge pile of straw on the right. The belt running from the threshing machine is probably linked to a steam engine. Threshing separated the grain from the straw and involved much hard, hot labor. *(Courtesy Buchanan District Library)*

John H. Wynn home. *(Courtesy Buchanan District Library)*

John H. Wynn. *(Courtesy Buchanan District Library)*

Mr. and Mrs. Fred Andrews in a playful pose aboard a one-horse cart. *(Courtesy Buchanan District Library)*

Attorney Alison Cress Roe and a pair of horses. Roe and his wife, Ruth, lived at 309 Front Street in Buchanan. *(Courtesy Buchanan District Library)*

Jay Glover, Sr., on a sickle mower. Glover owned a large farm west of Buchanan by Weaver Lake. *(Courtesy Buchanan District Library)*

The Frank A. Stryker fruit farm at 409 River Street, ca. 1910. May Stryker, his wife, stands at center with a horse. *(Courtesy Buchanan District Library)*

Unidentified farmhouse and barn, ca. 1900. *(Courtesy Buchanan District Library)*

William Lyddick in a stylish buggy, posed in front of an even more stylish barn, ca. 1910. Lyddick had a 120 acre farm in Bertrand Township. Farmers like Lyddick took great pride in their barns. *(Courtesy Buchanan District Library)*

The John Parrot farm. *(Courtesy Buchanan District Library)*

A dinner and Chautauqua at the Buchanan school, August 23, 1913. The Chautauqua Movement brought educational programs, culture and entertainment into rural communities like Buchanan. *(Courtesy Buchanan District Library)*

William H. and Minnie Ingalls, with Mae (Jaeger) Bates, at their house about a mile west of Buchanan, ca. 1913. *(Courtesy Buchanan District Library)*

Chapter 4
Downtown

A city's downtown business district defines its image in the popular imagination. People identify Chicago, for example, with its famous "Loop" area, not its outlying suburbs, and New York City with the Manhattan skyline. Regardless of the city's size or the variety of buildings in the surrounding areas, the downtown fixes its image in the mind's eye. The downtown retail district has defined Buchanan as well.

Buchanan's downtown grew up along Front Street and stretched north along Main, no doubt in accordance with John Hamilton's intended plan. Roads throughout the region converged on Front Street in Buchanan, leading to the street's development as a market center. The Niles-Buchanan Road (which became Front Street when it reached Buchanan) enjoyed particular importance, for it linked Buchanan with the larger town of Niles, five miles distant. The Michigan Central Railroad on the south edge of town brought manufactured goods to Buchanan and shipped out agricultural produce from the area's farms, flour and lumber from local mills, and finished goods from Buchanan industries. The shops along Front Street catered to the farmers who had come to town with grain for the mills, loggers bringing in wood for lumber, and village residents needing to do shopping. Everyone headed for Front Street.

The Front Street business district was already well developed by 1860. A plat map published that year listed numerous shops in town. People could stop at George Dutton's grocery or Hiram N. Mowrey's blacksmith shop. H. B. Knight and Garrett Morris dealt in produce and Charles Clark ran the town hardware. General merchandise could be had at the shops of Ross, Alexander & Co., Daniel Terriere and T. L. Rose & Company. A trip to town sometimes necessitated an overnight stay for people who lived well outside of the village. Those needing accommodations could find rooms at the town's first hotel, which Garrett Morris built in 1846 and sold about ten years later to Russell McCoy. By 1860, visitors could also stay at J. N. Post's American Hotel. The town's first newspaper appeared in 1858 with the publication of the *Buchanan Vindicator,* edited by J. N. Potter. This pro-Republican paper attracted few subscribers, and in 1862 it was absorbed by the *Buchanan Weekly Union.* Daniel A. Wagner bought the paper in 1866, and the following year changed its name to the *Berrien County Record.* Other newspapers challenged the *Record,* including *The Independent,* the *Buchanan National,* the *Buchanan Argus* and the *Buchanan Reporter,* but none survived for any length of time. The *Record* continues in publication at this writing, and is the oldest business enterprise in the city.

John D. Ross and Lorenzo Alexander's three-story "Excelsior Block," built in 1858, was the town's most prominent building. In nineteenth century parlance, a "block" referred to a multi-story building with retail space on the first floor and offices or apartments on the upper floors. In the Excelsior Block, Buchanan could boast one of the finest such blocks in Berrien County. To Americans of that era, brick construction signified prosperity and permanence – a sign that a town had grown out of its frontier beginnings and taken its place among the nation's established communities. In 1862, Ross and Alexander built a second brick block on the south side of Front Street, which in a nod to Civil War patriotism they christened the "Union Block." A devastating fire swept Buchanan on October 31, 1862, and leveled the Excelsior Block just as the Union Block neared completion. Buchanan's continued prosperity with its solid industrial base, however, ensured that merchants replaced their wooden buildings in the downtown with brick structures.

Buchanan's numerous mills and factories generated employment and income for village residents, and this relative wealth manifested itself in the constantly growing downtown. By the early 1870s, stores lined both sides of Front Street between Oak Street and Days Avenue, and continued for another block along North Main Street. Visitors had their choice of lodging at Stephen Dann's Tremont House on the corner of Oak and Front, the Dunbar House on Ferry and Lyon or the Niagara House on North Main. They could stable their horses or rent a team at either of two liveries. Five different stores sold groceries and dry goods. Binns & Rose carried dry goods and general merchandise, Solomon L. Estes sold "Ready made Clothing and Gent's furnishing goods," and J. J. Howe's store had "Dry goods, Clothing, Carpets, Hats, Caps, Groceries, Crockery and Glassware, and General Merchandise." The hardware store of Collins & Weaver carried all kinds of hardware, stoves and paint. T. J. Jones operated a barbershop and bathhouse, where one could luxuriate in "Warm and Cold Baths at all times" – a luxury in an era generally bereft of indoor plumbing.

Photographic portraits could be had at Marvin Cathcart's photography studio on Main Street. LeRoy Dodd made liver pills and "Dodd's Cough Balsam" (a patent medicine possessed of dubious curative powers) on Front Street. Mrs. Philander B. Dunning ran a millinery and hoop skirt shop on Main Street. W. F. Molsberry had a billiard hall and bowling alley on Front Street.

Buchanan's population grew at a steady pace through the mid-nineteenth century. By 1884, 2,070 people lived in Buchanan; only Niles and St. Joseph ranked larger among Berrien County's towns, with Benton Harbor trailing a distant fourth. The village's population actually dipped slightly at the beginning of the twentieth century, dropping to 1,831 in 1910. The population loss may have come about in part through the closure of some of the town's factories around that time, forcing Buchanan workers to leave town to seek jobs in other communities. Employment at Clark Equipment Company, however, revitalized Buchanan. By 1920, the town's population had grown to 3,187 people, an increase of over 57% in just ten years. Buchanan's population continued to climb during the mid-20th century, numbering 3,922 people in 1930, 4,057 in 1940 and 4,645 in 1970.

Business listings in Buchanan during the early 20th century illustrate the great variety of retail businesses in the town. Travel to other towns took too long for shopping trips, but stores in Buchanan offered nearly everything the residents wanted or needed. Brooks Shoe Store sold boots and shoes. The firm of Lundgren & Allen still sold "Buggies, Wagons, Harness and All Kinds of Agricultural Implements" and two blacksmith shops (Miles & Boyer and Elmer Remington) still operated in town, but Herbert G. Roe had gone into the automotive business – a harbinger of things to come. Residents had their choice of three dry goods stores, a drug store and eight groceries, and could buy fruit and produce Cascarelli Brothers. Women's hats were still much in vogue, and ladies could shop from three milliners: Orma Chamberlain, Esther Parkinson, and the Paris Hat Shop. Luxuries were available, too. Two jewelers had shops in town – H. E. Lough and Ray W. Johnson – and flowers could be had from Dana L. Rough. Amusements abounded in the downtown as well. Four ice cream fountains, including Lyddick's Ice Cream Parlor and the curiously named Sanitary Sweet Shop, catered to people's hunger for sweets. Three pool halls (often frowned upon by the better class of society), offered billiards and pool. All in all, Buchanan's citizens could find nearly everything they desired right in their own hometown.

The Buchanan Public Library originated about 1915 with a few shelves of books in the township clerk's office on Main Street. Township Clerk Irene Sparks checked out books for patrons in between her other duties. This library eventually went defunct, but a successor opened about 1936 on the north side of Front Street. About 1941, library operations moved into a small room in the Buchanan City Hall. The library finally obtained its own building with the construction of an entirely new facility on West Front Street in 1955-1956. The Reinke Construction Company erected the structure, which was dedicated on June 17, 1956. A 1,500 square foot addition went up in 1965-1966, followed by another addition in 1979.

Steady employment at Clark Equipment, Electro-Voice and other manufacturers in the 1950s fueled consumer spending and contributed to the health of downtown businesses. Buchanan residents enjoyed a thriving retail sector. Retail shops, especially those on Front Street, did a good business with city residents and people from the surrounding rural areas that came into town to shop. Basic necessities, including groceries, medicines, dry goods and hardware all could be found in Buchanan. City directories list sixteen different grocery stores in the city, most notably the A & P at 117 N. Portage, S & S Super Market at 101 Days Avenue, and Thompson's I. G. A. on West Front Street. Desenberg's Men's Store, Koenigshof's Dry Goods, and the Roti Roti Shoe Store, among others, supplied dry goods, and people could pick up medical prescriptions at Wisner's Corner Drug Store or Grodtke Drug Store, both on Front Street. Five lumberyards supplied building materials, including Buchanan Co-ops in the old Pears Mill building, Buchanan Lumber on Oak Street, and the Miller Lumber Company. Numerous automobile dealerships and auto parts shops served the community, including the Main Street Garage, Bowman's Garage and Buchanan Auto Supply. Buchananites could buy autos from Wisner Motor Sales (Plymouths, DeSotos and Jaguars), Frank Edmond (Chevrolets), Kennedy Motors (Buicks and Pontiacs), and Robert F. Habicht (Fords).

Downtown Buchanan entered an era of decline in the late 20th century. As happened in many small towns, retail stores began to disappear from Buchanan's downtown. The convenient transportation between urban centers that had done so much to invigorate Buchanan's commercial and industrial life began to draw business away from Front Street. Shopping trips to other, larger, towns like Niles and South Bend no longer meant interminable drives over bad roads, interspersed by a flat tire or two along the way. Instead, paved roads and better quality automobiles put once-distant shopping centers within a few minutes' drive of Buchanan. A 2003 study revealed that only 4% of Buchanan residents do most of their family shopping in town; South Bend, Mishawaka or Niles draw 94% of them, siphoning money away from their city's retailers. In an attempt to lure customers away from shopping malls, many business owners tried to modernize their 19th century storefronts with the latest in metal cladding and synthetic additions. A disagreeable stylistic hodgepodge resulted, diminishing Front Street's small town charm and further eroding the retail district's appeal. Many businesses that remained in Buchanan moved to the east side of the city, away from the downtown. The closure of Clark Equipment and other manufacturers cut into the city's economic base, as the city's residents had less money in their pockets to spend. Unable to survive, storeowners closed up shop. Empty storefronts dotted the downtown.

In recent years, Buchanan has made a concerted effort to revitalize its downtown. What have become known as "quality of life" attributes have become an important characteristic of the city. Many civic and governmental leaders have embraced the philosophy that people will want to live in a city that already offers attractive amenities, such as theaters, libraries and parks rather than waiting for a growing economy to generate those attractions. People have initiated numerous projects and organizations that have combined to make Buchanan a desirable town in which to live. The Tin Shop Theater offers live dramatic performance in its annual season, and the Buchanan Preservation Society's Pears Mill draws tourists with its interpretation of the historic gristmill. The Buchanan Public Library has become the Buchanan District Library. In 2002, it moved from its old building on Front Street into the vacant, and much larger, Electro-Voice building at the corner of Days Avenue and Front Street

The consulting firm of HyattPalma, Inc., helped the City of Buchanan create a study and plan for the downtown in 2003. Among other things, the plan calls for the restoration of the historic commercial architecture, along with historically-appropriate business signs to give the downtown a unified, aesthetically-pleasing appearance. The Buchanan Park along with downtown improvements to the sidewalks in 2004 has made the city more aesthetically attractive and friendlier to pedestrians. Buchanan's innovation, proactive stance toward revitalization has fostered an optimistic outlook in the city as it enters the 21st century.

Front Street decorated for Independence Day celebrations on July 4, 1881. A Civil War veterans reunion coincided with these celebrations and lasted for three days. The Trement House Hotel is pictured at the far left corner - one of the rare views of the hotel. *(Courtesy Buchanan District Library)*

Front Street, in this picture, is still dirt with wood boardwalks and crosswalks. Fire hydrants can be seen on the left side of the street and street lights hang above the center of the street. ca. 1905. *(Courtesy Buchanan District Library)*

In this view of Front Street, looking west, the familiar street lights as well as fire hydrants on the sidewalks can be seen. The old Michigan Bell telephone logo hangs on a building to the left. Dodd's Drug Store and a barber shop are in the right foreground. *(Courtesy Buchanan District Library)*

A congested day on Front Street. ca. 1905. *(Courtesy Buchanan District Library)*

Front street, looking east, has street lights installed by this time. The street is still dirt but has wood crosswalks installed so the pedestrian can avoid walking through dirt and mud. On the right side of the street you can see the businesses of Hutch's Confectionery and Ice Cream Parlor, Van Meter's bakery, Boardman and East. *(Courtesy Buchanan District Library)*

Large parade going down Front Street. You can see the store of "Morris the Fair, Dealer in Almost Everything," along with J. C. Scott store beside it on the right side. *(Courtesy Buchanan District Library)*

Homecoming parade going down Front Street, September 1910. *(Courtesy Buchanan District Library)*

Homecoming event on September 25, 1910 on Front Street. Note the temporary arch over Days Avenue. *(Courtesy Buchanan District Library)*

A crowded Days Avenue for the Homecoming on September 25, 1910. *(Courtesy Buchanan District Library)*

View of Front Street looking east. On the right side of the street you can see Hutch's Confectionery and Ice Cream Parlor. The Post Office and a bakery are on the left side of the street. *(Courtesy Buchanan District Library)*

View of Front Street. Note that the street is bricked at the time of this photo. *(Courtesy Buchanan District Library)*

Front Street, ca. 1953. *(Dale E. Florey Collection)*

Front Street, ca. 1957. *(Dale E. Florey Collection)*

View of Main Street looking north. Hosmer Photography Studio was on the second floor of the right hand corner building. Lee Bros. Bank was in the first floor of the corner building. Front Street is brick whereas Main Street is still dirt. *(Courtesy Buchanan District Library)*

An early view of Main Street looking north from Front Street. *(Courtesy Buchanan District Library)*

The dirt Main Street has wood crosswalks and sports numerous businesses on both sides of the street. You can make out Mrs. Esther Parkinson's Millinery Shop and the Cottage Hotel on the left side and the Harness Shop on the right side. *(Courtesy Buchanan District Library)*

Esther Parkinson standing with her dog in front of her millinery shop *(Courtesy Buchanan District Library)*

MILLINERY

A group of ladies posed outside a millinery shop. *(Courtesy Buchanan District Library)*

Days Avenue looking south from Front Street. *(Courtesy Buchanan District Library)*

Early view of Days Avenue when the street was still dirt. *(Courtesy Buchanan District Library)*

View of Days Avenue just prior to paving. *(Courtesy Buchanan District Library)*

McCollum Livery and Feed Stable. *(Courtesy Buchanan District Library)*

Livery Stable, 1895. *(Dale E. Florey Collection)*

View of McCoy's Creek with a livery barn on the right bank and Buchanan Mill in the background. *(Courtesy Buchanan District Library)*

A snowy day on McCoy's Creek. On October 10, 1906, twelve inches of snow fell and blanketed the village of Buchanan. *(Courtesy Buchanan District Library)*

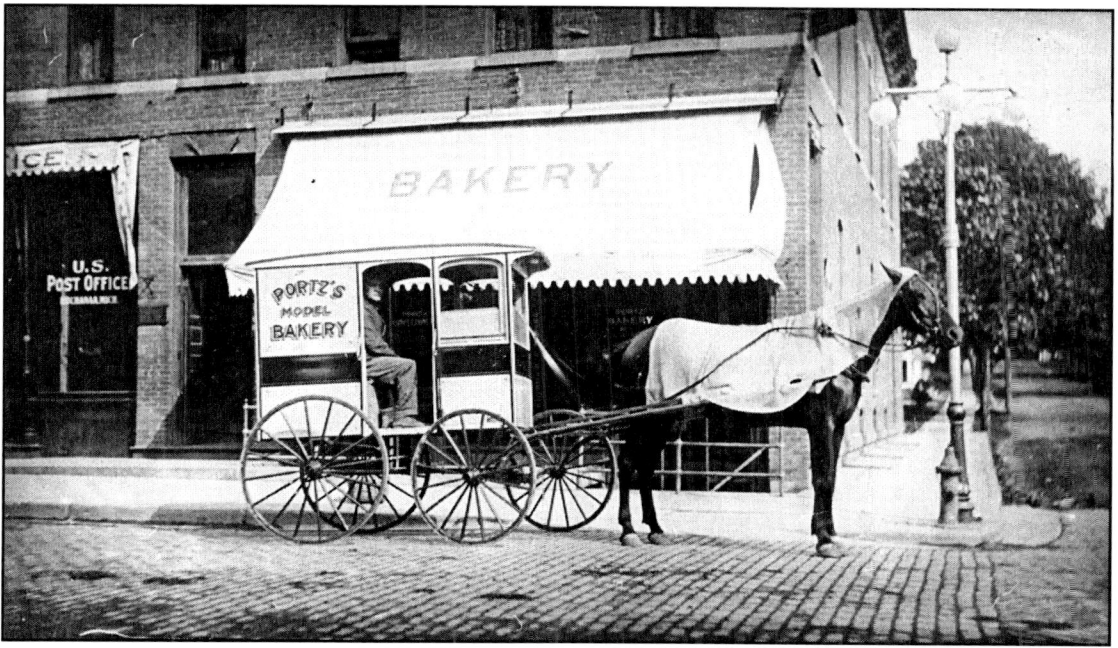

View of McCoy's Creek with a livery barn on the right bank. *(Courtesy Buchanan District Library)*

Portz's Bakery, ca. 1910. *(Dale E. Florey Collection)*

Hotel Buchanan at the corner of Days and Front streets. Looking east on Front Street, the Hollywood Theater can be seen. *(Dale E. Florey Collection)*

Sexton's Store. *(Dale E. Florey Collection)*

Unveiling the Memorial Fountain Clock on August 23, 1913. The banner across the street indicated a Chautauqua event was also planned. *(Courtesy Buchanan District Library)*

1913 Memorial Clock standing at the street corner in front of Ellsworth Pharmacy. Ellsworth in a white shirt and tie can be seen partially hidden on the left side by the clock. The Barber Shop (and baths), and H. C. Eisele Real Estate office can also be seen on the right side of the street. *(Courtesy Buchanan District Library)*

The memorial clock was installed in 1913 and the first floor stonework around the corner building had been installed sometime after 1913. *(Courtesy Buchanan District Library)*

Hotel Earl, located at the corner of Front Street and Day Avenue, was razed in 1961. A new building was built by Clark Equipment Credit Corporation and later occupied by Electro-Voice Company. Today the Buchanan District Library occupies the building that replaced Hotel Earl. Bird's Omnibus Line is parked in front of the hotel to pick up passengers. *(Courtesy Buchanan District Library)*

The Cottage Hotel, also known as the American House Hotel, was located on Main Street about two blocks north of Front Street. *(Courtesy Donald F. Ryman)*

The Cottage Hotel. *(Courtesy Buchanan District Library)*

Cigar and tobacco shop, ca. 1957. *(Dale E. Florey Collection)*

Excavating the Niles-Buchanan Gas Line, September 4, 1913. *(Courtesy Buchanan District Library)*

Interior of William N. Broderick's Drug Store, ca. 1910. *(Courtesy Buchanan District Library)*

Interior of Broderick Drug Store. The poster is promoting Berrien County Young People's picnic in Berrien Springs on August 6, 1902. *(Courtesy Buchanan District Library)*

Interior of the Broderick Drug Store. The store is lit by electric lights in this night scene. *(Courtesy Buchanan District Library)*

G. E. Smith & Co. The G. E. Smith store was a general merchantile with fresh fruits and vegetables being showcased in exterior bins. Glen E. Smith stands at far right in the doorway. *(Courtesy Buchanan District Library)*

Hello Central. . . ! The Buchanan telephone exchange, ca. 1905. Men, left to right: Virgil Schwartz, John Morris and Oscar Morris. Women, left to right: M. Wagner, E. Tabor and Edna Kean. *(Courtesy Buchanan District Library)*

William A. Sparks stands in front of his Shaving Parlor. *(Courtesy Buchanan District Library)*

Interior of barber shop with William Sparks (left) and Charles Diggins (right). *(Courtesy Buchanan District Library)*

Interior of barber shop. From left to right: Clare Coveney, Ernie Fox (center rear), Ted Rouse and Fulton Powers. *(Courtesy Buchanan District Library)*

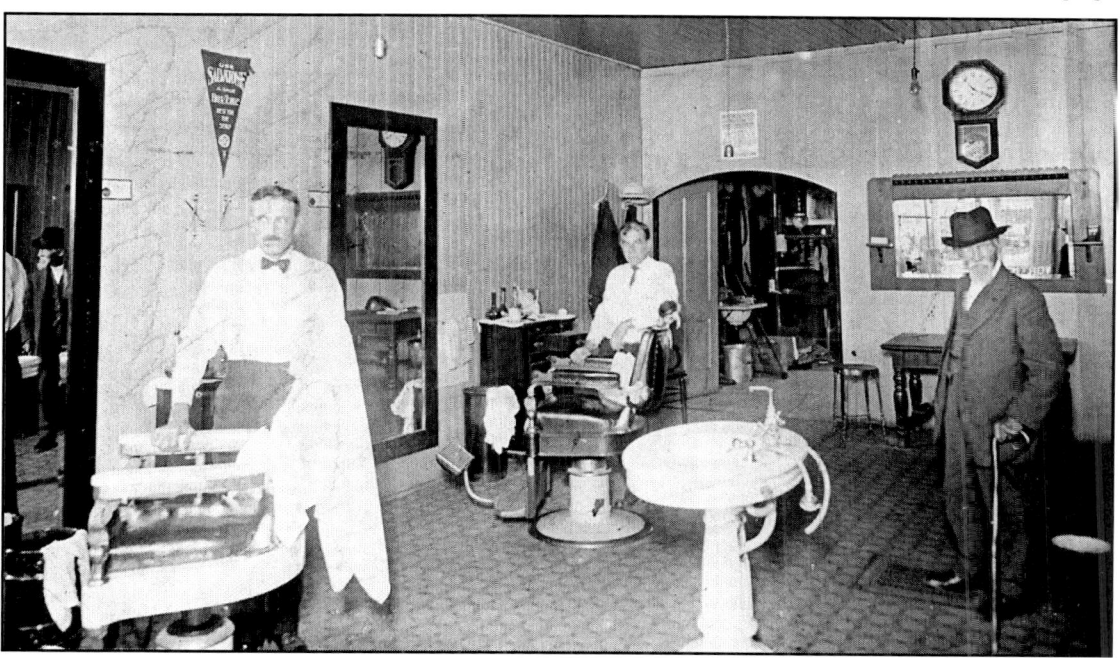

Interior of barber shop. Pictured from left to right are Ted Rouse, Gene Murphy and Judge Charles E. Sabin. *(Courtesy Buchanan District Library)*

Portrait of an older Ted Rouse. *(Courtesy Buchanan District Library)*

Lyddick Stevens Confectionery. Pictured from left to right are Messrs. Charles E. Lyddick, Hutchinson, and Stevens. *(Courtesy Buchanan District Library)*

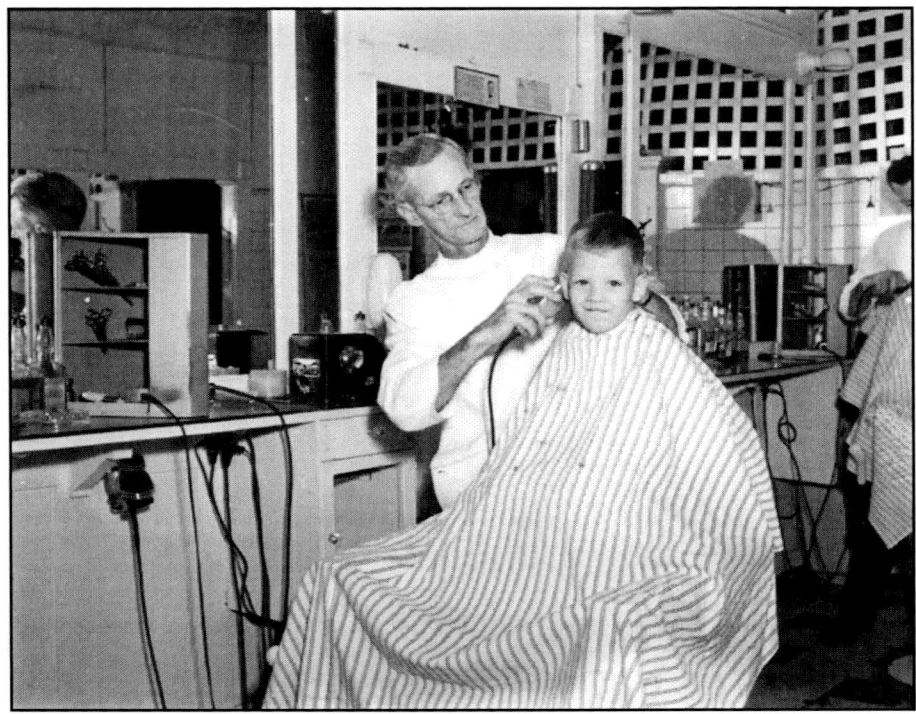

A youngster sits patiently as Marlin Kean cuts his hair, ca. 1965. *(Courtesy Berrien County Record)*

Lyddick Ice Cream Parlor at 104 E. Front Street. Typical confectioneries sold ice cream as well as other sweets, confectioneries and gifts. Charles Lyddick at the counter also offered confectioneries for the sweet tooth, cigars, pennants, and stationery. *(Courtesy Buchanan District Library)*

Photo of Herm Davis, delivery driver for C. D. Kent Grocery. Rare photo of an African American in early Buchanan. *(Courtesy Buchanan District Library)*

Interior of Donley Brothers Cigar Store. *(Courtesy Buchanan District Library)*

Interior of Boardman-Wherle Grocery. From left to right: Boardman, unidentified, Smith, and Wherle at far right sporting the white apron. *(Courtesy Buchanan District Library)*

Henry R. Adams Hardware Store. Standing in the doorway from left to right are John Wynn, Jr. and Fred Poyser. Seated at the left side of the bench is Henry Grice. The other man is unidentified. *(Courtesy Buchanan District Library)*

H. E. Lough (left) posing in front of his store H. E. Lough Jewelry Shop, ca. 1910. Notice that the building has the sign of J. H. Roe, Jeweler above the doorway. *(Courtesy Buchanan District Library)*

Boardman-Wherle Grocery. *(Courtesy Buchanan District Library)*

Herbert G. Roe and Charles W. Landis (cashiers) at the Lee Bank, ca. 1915. *(Courtesy Buchanan District Library)*

Interior of Stauffer Grocery Store. *(Courtesy Buchanan District Library)*

Batchelor Livery Barn. Herb Batchelor is the third person from the right (with the "x" above his head) wearing a coat and tie. *(Courtesy Buchanan District Library)*

Interior of Smith Shoe Store. Walter Shoop is standing at the left with Glen E. Smith to the right. The women are unidentified. *(Courtesy Buchanan District Library)*

Unidentified Batchelor Livery Barn workers. *(Courtesy Buchanan District Library)*

Marble Hardware store was located in the Redden Block on Front Street. *(Courtesy Buchanan District Library)*

Interior of E. S. Roe Hardware Store. *(Courtesy Buchanan District Library)*

Harry Beistle and his popcorn cart. *(Courtesy Buchanan District Library)*

[Left] A group photo of the *Berrien County Record* staff in 1876. Unfortunately they are not identified. *(Courtesy Buchanan District Library)*

Portrait of Clyde Baker, owner of Baker Dry Goods Store. *(Courtesy Buchanan District Library)*

Interior of Clyde Baker Dry Goods Store, November 1893. *(Courtesy Buchanan District Library)*

Clyde H. Baker Dry Goods Store all decked out with U.S. flags. *(Courtesy Buchanan District Library)*

Interior of Sam Smith's Cigar Store. *(Courtesy Buchanan District Library)*

Cook & Sands Meat Market. Bill Cook holds up a prime cut of meat to a female customer with Nate Sands standing to the right. *(Courtesy Buchanan District Library)*

Nate Sands Market. An older Nate Sands stands in the center with white apron. *(Courtesy Buchanan District Library)*

Interior of Merson Meat Market, 1924. Dan Merson poses at his counter. *(Courtesy Buchanan District Library)*

Art Mahew, undated. *(Courtesy Berrien County Record)*

Grand opening of the S. and S. Supermarket, June 23, 1955. *(Courtesy Berrien County Record)*

Buchanan's first motion picture theater, ca. 1915. Theater owner Phay Graffort in white shirt) stands in the doorway at left, while his wife Martha ("Mattie") sells tickets at the box office window. The two-reel feature *Under Fire* is the upcoming attraction. *(Courtesy Buchanan District Library)*

Interior of Jake Baker's Harness Shop. From left to right: Jake Baker (behind the counter), unidentified customer, Harry Hanover, Alvin Rokely *(Courtesy Buchanan District Library)*

[Left] Portrait of Jake Baker, harness maker. Note the Grand Army of the Republic (G.A.R.) ribbon pinned to his chest. *(Courtesy Buchanan District Library)*

[Right] This person is identified as the first Chinese laundry man but his name is unknown. In the latter part of the nineteenth century, Buchanan had a Chinese laundry owned by Charley Gong. *(Courtesy Buchanan District Library)*

Barber's shoe repair shop. *(Courtesy Buchanan District Library)*

The Harness Shop.
Pictured are Ned Cook
and his father.
*(Courtesy Buchanan
District Library)*

Roe's Bakery. Pictured from left to right are: _____, Nellie Cathcart, Mr. Raven, Al Emmerson and Bertha Roe. *(Courtesy Buchanan District Library)*

Interior of Rehm's Racket Store. *(Courtesy Buchanan District Library)*

The Racket Store. J. C. Rehm, owner, poses in front of his store. *(Courtesy Buchanan District Library)*

Interior of D's Café. Pictured are wait staff and other employees. *(Courtesy Buchanan District Library)*

Beck's Market. Harry Beck, with cigar, stands behind the counter. *(Courtesy Buchanan District Library)*

Smith Cigar Store. Sam Smith stands in front of his store. Note the wooden cigar store Indian at the right. *(Courtesy Buchanan District Library)*

Group standing in front of early electric office. *(Courtesy Buchanan District Library)*

Treat Buildings at 211 East Front Street, ca. 1952. Willis Treat built the building in 1924 as a grocery store. Watson's grocery store was located in the single story section at the far left. The Berrien County Record newspaper was located in the center portion. *(Courtesy Buchanan District Library)*

H. R. Adams Hardware Store. Henry R. Adams poses in the doorway. His storefront window also indicates he retails wagons and harnesses too. *(Courtesy Buchanan District Library)*

Interior view of Harry Boyce Garage. *(Courtesy Buchanan District Library)*

Interior of Miles Blacksmith Shop, owned by Burgess Miles. *(Courtesy Buchanan District Library)*

Fay Wilcox at the counter of his Cigar Store. *(Courtesy Buchanan District Library)*

Sparks and Hathaway Building Fire of 1892. The temperature was 16 degrees below zero and hampered the firefighters ability to put out the fire. *(Courtesy Buchanan District Library)*

Swem Funeral Home. *(Courtesy Buchanan District Library)*

Interior of dry goods store. Pictured from left to right are Mr. Severson and John Ham. *(Courtesy Buchanan District Library)*

McCollum Livery and Feed Stable. *(Courtesy Buchanan District Library)*

E. E. Remington Blacksmith Shop. Pictured outside the shop from left to right are Paul Wynn, Elmer E. Remington, _____, _____, Hiriam Mowrey. *(Courtesy Buchanan District Library)*

Interior of (Elmer E.) Remington Blacksmith Shop. *(Courtesy Buchanan District Library)*

Interior of either a dry goods store or drug store. Pictured at far left is Mrs. Fuller. *(Courtesy Buchanan District Library)*

Two young drivers test drive the year's current model automobiles, ca. 1955. *(Courtesy Berrien County Record)*

Sinclair Gas Station, ca. 1963. *(Dale E. Florey Collection)*

Louie Poplar owned the Phillips 66 station. The Trophy House is currently on the old
Phillips 66 site. Photo ca. 1955. *(Courtesy Berrien County Record)*

Forrest Blood, ca. 1960. *(Courtesy Berrien County Record)*

Standard Gas Station. The tall man pictured second from the left is Ike Koloff. *(Courtesy Buchanan District Library)*

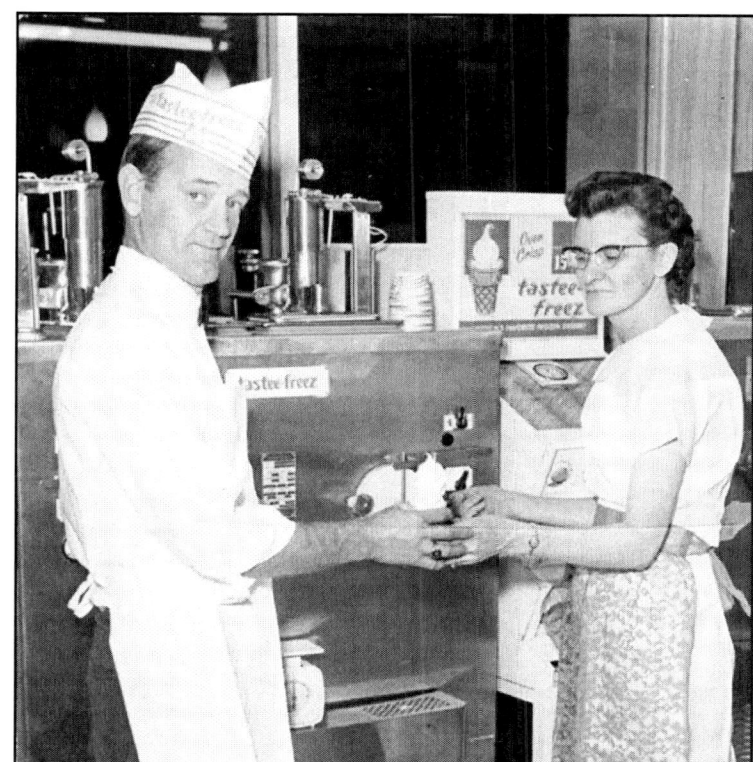

James and Nina Kepler, ca. 1963. *(Courtesy Eerrien County Record)*

Herb Kley shows a display of firearms for sale, ca. 1955. *(Courtesy Berrien County Record)*

The Buchanan Post Office in 1906. Left to right: James Scott, _____ Ingalls, Flora Currier, Postmaster Albert A. Worthington, Tennyson E. Van Every, Edwin W. Ashbrook and William Rose. *(Courtesy Buchanan Distric Library)*

The postal staff at work, 1915. Left to right: Postmaster Jacob Rough, Tennyson E. Van Every and Flora Currier. *(Courtesy Buchanan Distric Library)*

Chapter 5
Domestic Architecture

Greek Revival, Italianate, Gothic Revival, Queen Anne, Classical Revival, Craftsman, Bungalow – Buchanan has them all. Domestic architecture flourished in Buchanan during the nineteenth and early twentieth century. The town's industries produced wealth for their owners, which they showcased in their homes. Fine homes, built with taste, skilled craftsmanship and the best materials, sprang up all over Buchanan. As a result, the city boasted some of the best domestic architecture in southwest Michigan. Most of the grandest homes were built on West Front Street, where their owners could display their sophistication (and wealth) to the world.

Popular images of frontier Michigan feature pioneer settlers sitting at fireplace hearths in their rustic log cabins. Smoke curls out the chimney and the latchstring hangs out the door in a welcome to visitors. The image is largely myth – not entirely false, for a few settlers did indeed build log cabins, but still an inaccurate if pleasant picture of Michigan's early homes.

The first history of Berrien County, published in 1880 when the old-time pioneer residents could still tell their stories, reported several log cabins constructed in the Buchanan area. One of the first settlers, Charles Cowles, a cabinetmaker from Vermont, built a cabin there in the summer of 1834. He liked the area so well that he stayed for the rest of his life, living in Buchanan Township until his death in 1885 at age 81. The same book recounts the building of a few other log cabins around Buchanan, including those of Russell McCoy and Hiram Wray in 1834 and Hiram Weese in 1840.

Most of Buchanan's early residents, however, chose the Greek Revival style of architecture for their first homes in Michigan. Although log cabins were not a rarity, homes that harkened back to the architecture of ancient Greece enjoyed much greater popularity. The area's first settlers emigrated from New York and New England. Accustomed to stylish homes built of wood, brick or stone, they wanted the same type of house they had enjoyed back East. They viewed log cabins with disdain and built them only as temporary shelter. Greek Revivals, however, duplicated the familiar homes that they had left behind. Enormously popular from about 1830 to 1860, Greek Revival was also known as the National Style for its predominance in America. The design attempted to emulate the form and details of ancient Greek architecture, the Parthenon in Athens being the ideal. Many outstanding examples of the style appeared in Buchanan, and many survive to the present time. The Thomas L. Ross House on Front Street (ca. 1859) exists in almost pristine condition, including most of the original interior. The John D. Ross House (1856), also on Front Street, is best known to town residents as the old City Hall; despite a remodeling in 1879 that gave it some Queen Anne elements, it survives in good condition as one of the town's oldest Greek Revival homes. Still another fine example of the Greek Revival style can be seen in the beautifully restored home of Peter and Mary Lysy on Moccasin Street.

The Gothic Revival style of the 1830-1860 period romanticized the architecture of medieval Europe. Sir Walter Scott's novel *Ivanhoe* and the interpretive designs advanced by influential American architect Andrew Jackson Downing helped popularize the style. Although not nearly as common as Greek Revival or the later Italianate style (and relatively rare elsewhere in Berrien County), Gothic Revival architecture saw frequent use in both Buchanan and Niles. Architects and builders most often applied the design to churches, but its steeply pitched roofline, gingerbread vergeboard and pointed arches appeared in domestic architecture as well. A few Gothic Revival homes remain in Buchanan, but all have been significantly altered and retain little of their original charm.

From around 1860 until the late 1880s, the Italianate style reigned supreme. The

Greek and Gothic Revival styles faded from popularity in the 1850s and early 1860s. The Italianate style enjoyed enormous popularity throughout the Midwest, and Buchanan was no exception. Buchanan mirrored America's changing taste in architecture and its residents embraced the new styles coming into fashion. Domestic and commercial buildings of both brick and wood frame construction went up in the new style, and dozens of fine examples remain in Buchanan to this day. The style developed an architectural theme loosely derived from Italian country villas – Italy then being considered the pinnacle of culture and sophistication.

Notable Italianate houses in Buchanan include a string of palatial homes erected on stylish West Front Street. Thomas M. Fulton, president of the First National Bank of Buchanan, built his home at 203 West Front in 1865 for $25,000 – this at a time when one could build a quite respectable wood frame house for $500. A year later, wagon manufacturer Jacob B. Luther built an opulent brick home with a four-story tower at 118 W. Front. William Pears' Italianate mansion at 303 W. Front could challenge residences everywhere for splendor. Probably built in the late 1860s for Pears, a mill owner, the brick residence featured a Second Empire-style mansard roof that was unfortunately destroyed by fire in 1922. Other fine Italianates on Buchanan's "Millionaire's Row" included the Charles Clark House (1867); the Lorenzo P. Alexander House (ca. 1865); and the Leander P. Fox House (ca. 1865), built for a partner in the Zinc Collar Pad Company. All of the grand Italianate homes on Front Street still stand in varying degrees of preservation except the Fox House.

The Italianate style fell from favor during the 1880s as the Queen Anne style came into fashion. Americans often associate the Queen Anne style with "Victorian" houses: a steeply pitched, gabled roof; asymmetrical shape; large porches with gingerbread decoration; and frequently a round turret on the side. The style name comes from a supposed resemblance to English rural architecture of the early eighteenth century, in the time of Queen Anne, but the style is actually derived from a variety of elements of English country houses over a wide range of time periods. Buchananites built many Queen Anne houses. A notable example stands at 309 West Front Street, built in 1884 for a prominent attorney Alison C. Roe. Another Queen Anne residence, the Amos C. House home, was built about 1893 on the southwest corner of Front and Oak Streets. Unfortunately, it was razed in the late 1960s. Still another example of the Queen Anne style, the 1884 Jacob Imhoff House, stands on South Detroit Street.

The early twentieth century saw scores of Bungalow and American Foursquare homes built in Buchanan. The Bungalow style developed in California and soon spread across America. These single-story houses featured gently pitched broad gables. A lower gable usually covered a porch, while the larger, upper gable covered the main structure. The American Foursquare, common throughout Michigan and other Midwest states, also appeared frequently in Buchanan. The simple, comfortable Foursquare was essentially a two-story box surmounted by a hipped roof. Bungalows and Foursquares were often purchased as prefabricated kit houses from Sears, Roebuck or the Aladdin Company of Bay City, Michigan. Builders bought kit homes through a catalog, just as one could order clothing or hardware. Shipped via railroad (the Michigan Central offered ideal freight service to Buchanan), the kit houses came complete with everything needed, from studs and rafters to doors, windows and even paint.

California's influence in the Midwest continued after World War II in the ubiquitous single-story Ranch style house. The Ranch house epitomized the ideals of "useful and practical." Gone were the elaborate cornices and window hoods of the Italianates and the gingerbread of the Queen Annes, scorned as unnecessary frills. The modernistic Ranch houses instead stressed simplicity and clean lines.

Insufficient housing to meet the community's needs became a continual problem for Buchanan during the twentieth century. The number of employees at Clark Equipment

Company grew at a rate that outpaced the available housing stock. As the town's population soared, Buchanan added new subdivisions to shelter the influx of workers. In 1918, Clark organized the Buchanan Land Company with $100,000 in capital. It bought a farm on the west side of town just off the Niles-Buchanan Road, platted it into lots, planted trees, and built houses that ranged in price from $2,500 to $4,500. World War I patriotism gave Clark's new housing development its name: Liberty Heights. The Bungalow and American Foursquare styles predominated in Liberty Heights.

Buchanan's housing shortage became apparent during World War II as industries, especially Clark Equipment, hired in outside workers that they needed for war production. The federal government rationed virtually everything during the war, including building materials, and new construction needed special, hard-to-obtain permits. New arrivals in Buchanan lived in federally-operated trailer parks – segregated by race – in locations around Portage and Moccasin Streets. New subdivisions built after the war, including Colonial Gardens, Paden Park, Park Ridge and Samson Terrace, alleviated the town's housing shortage.

Today, many of Buchanan's grand old homes of the nineteenth and early twentieth century still survive. Later owners often "remuddled" these houses with synthetic siding and architecturally inappropriate additions. Buchanan's continued industry-generated wealth put money in homeowners' pockets. This gave them the means to alter their homes in an effort to give them a more modern appearance – usually with unfortunate results. Other houses were demolished and lost to the community forever. In recent years, however, Buchanan has emerged as an area leader in historic preservation with a progressive outlook on its domestic architecture. The Buchanan Preservation Society has restored and opened the Pears Mill in the downtown and fostered preservation awareness in the residential areas. Its leaders, including Donald and Martha Ryman, William Cameron, Margaret Mitenbuler, Peter and Mary Lysy, Eric and Carol Hageman and others, have spearheaded preservation efforts and, in some cases, restored their own homes as examples to the rest of Berrien County.

The John D. Ross house on West Front Street may be Buchanan's best-known residence. Buchanan banker John Ross built the Greek Revival-style home in 1856, then remodeled it in 1879 by adding mansard roofs to the side wings and placing a portico across the facade. After Ross' death in 1888, his son Alfred F. Ross occupied the house until 1897. The families of Ephraim W. Sanders (a banker) and his son, Frank (an attorney), owned the house from 1897 to 1951, at which time the City of Buchanan bought it. It served as the Buchanan City Hall until 1984 and as the city police station. *(Courtesy Buchanan District Library)*

[102]

The John D. Ross house as it appeared in 1860, four years after its construction. (*Map of the Counties Cass, Van Buren and Berrien, Michigan,* 1860).

The Benjamin and Harriet Tomlinson log house, located north of Buchanan on section 15 off Miller Road. The house has obviously fallen into disrepair. Most Northerners never meant their log houses to last more than a few years. After they built a more "modern" home of frame or brick construction they converted their log houses into stables or sheds, or simply left them to rot away. *(Courtesy Buchanan District Library)*

The Matilda Estes home at 209 Main Street (corner of Main and Third streets), built in the distinctive Greek Revival style. The Estes family owned the house during the early 20th century, but it was built prior to 1860. *(Courtesy Buchanan District Library)*

The Charles Schuyler Black house, ca. 1880. The Italianate style house features intricate columns and scrollwork on the wraparound porch. It stood on the north side of Dewey (then Second) Avenue), midway between Oak and West streets. Charles, with his father Horace, ran the Black & Willard Furniture Company. The Vermont native lived in Buchanan until his death in 1913 at age 84. *(Courtesy Buchanan District Library)*

The home of Wellington W. Wells, pastor of Buchanan's Presbyterian Church during the 1870s. The house stood at 310 West Front Street. His son, Wellington S. Wells, lived next door at 312 West Front. *(Courtesy Buchanan District Library)*

The Bristol house's steeply pitched roof suggests the Gothic Revival style of architecture. The terne metal roof seen here, often referred to as a tin roof, was made of steel coated with an alloy of lead and tin. *(Courtesy Buchanan District Library)*

Known as the Charles Black "River House," the Charles Schuyler Black
house stood east of Buchanan near the St. Joseph River bridge. *(Courtesy
Buchanan District Library)*

The Charles Schuyler Black house at the St. Joseph River bridge, ca. 1900. The
house stood on the south side of River Street on the west side of the river. Note
the large stone by the gate to help travelers dismount from carriages. *(Courtesy
Buchanan District Library)*

River street near the St. Joseph River bridge, ca. 1910. The Charles S. Black home lay just across the river from this view. *(Courtesy Buchanan District Library)*

This unidentified house in the Buchanan area, built ca. 1890, had simple, elegant features. Note the "gingerbread" trim in the roof peak. *(Courtesy Buchanan District Library)*

The Marble family house on Fourth Street. *(Courtesy Buchanan District Library)*

The W. P. Hatch residence. *(Courtesy Buchanan District Library)*

Frank and Frances Imhoff owned this house on Portage Street. Frank worked as a grinder foreman at Clark Equipment. *(Courtesy Buchanan District Library)*

This elegant brick Italianate house belonged to Edward J. Long. Brick homes cost more money to build than wood-framed houses, but their long-term durability made up for the expense. *(Courtesy Buchanan District Library)*

A bucolic scene looking down the Fourth Street residential neighborhood, ca. 1910. The view could have come out of a Norman Rockwell painting, complete with children playing along the walks. *(Courtesy Buchanan District Library)*

Front Street residences, ca. 1910. The nearest house with its curved mansard roof is a fine example of the French Second Empire architectural style. Considered one of the "Picturesque" styles, Second Empire enjoyed great popularity in American from about 1860 to 1885. *(Courtesy Buchanan Preservation Society)*

An unidentified Buchanan-area farmhouse, ca. 1905. As the 20th century began, the multi-colored paint schemes of the Victorian era (often referred to today as "painted ladies") vanished, replaced by white. *(Courtesy Buchanan District Library)*

William Pears house at 303 West Front Street. Pears, a mill owner, built the magnificent Italianate house with a French Second Empire third story about 1866. A fire destroyed the two upper stories on October 13, 1922. *(Courtesy Buchanan District Library)*

A group posed around a house identified only as "the Scott home," ca. 1890. One of the window shutters, always a high maintenance item, has become detached. Victorian Americans loved decorative plantings, as indicated by those around this house. *(Courtesy Buchanan District Library)*

Residential street scene in Buchanan, ca. 1900. *(Courtesy Buchanan District Library)*

Storm damage at the Leander Perry Fox House, ca. 1880. Fox, who built the house about 1865, was a partner with George H. Richards in the Zinc Collar Pad Company, a business whose profits made him sufficiently wealthy to build this elegant Italianate house on West Front Street. Fox was also a leader in the Advent Christian Church. The house was razed about 1950 to make way for St. Paul's Lutheran Church and parsonage. *(Courtesy Buchanan District Library)*

Porter and Fred Andrews' homes in Buchanan, ca. 1910. *(Courtesy Buchanan District Library)*

Dr. William H. Landis became the second owner of the Leander P. Fox House, which stood on the northeast corner of West Front and Lake streets. By the time this photograph was taken around 1910, a larger Neo-Classical style porch with Doric columns had replaced the original Italianate porch. The automobile parked in front, which probably belonged to Dr. Landis, is a 1910 model Maxwell. *(Courtesy Buchanan District Library)*

The William D. Bremer home at 205 N. Front Street, ca. 1915. The house is a fine example of the Neo-Classical style, with Ionic columns supporting a broad front porch. *(Courtesy Buchanan District Library)*

The beautiful Front Street residential area, looking west from downtown. *(Courtesy Buchanan District Library)*

The home of George and Matilda Hanley at 204 West Front Street, ca. 1920. *(Courtesy Buchanan District Library)*

A Buchanan street scene. *(Courtesy Buchanan District Library)*

Andrew J. Carothers' home on the east side of the St. Joseph River. Carothers was born in Mishawaka, Indiana, in 1845, and served during the Civil War first as a teamster and, later, as a bugler in the 12th Indiana Cavalry. He moved to Buchanan in 1874, and ran the three-story Hotel Earl in downtown Buchanan during the 1890s. He also sold ice and operated the "Buchanan German Carp Ponds." *(Courtesy Buchanan District Library)*

One of Buchanan's residential neighborhoods, ca. 1930. Large shade trees not only beauti-fied the town, but also helped cool the homes in the days before air conditioning. *(Courtesy Buchanan District Library)*

William and Maggie Van Meter pose in front of their stylish house at 201 Clark Street in Buchanan, ca. 1910. Note the fishscale shingles in the roof peak and the "gingerbread" on the porch. William was a salesman. *(Courtesy Buchanan District Library)*

Dr. Berrick was born in Middlesex, Massachusetts, in 1823. As a young man, Berrick pursued a remarkable string of professional occupations. He entered the ministry of the Second Advent Church in 1847 and held pastorates in several churches. He enrolled in Harvard College's law department in 1859 and after being admitted to the bar in 1864 practiced law in Boston for two years. He returned to the ministry in 1868 when he moved to Minnesota and then to Indiana. He moved to Buchanan a year later, probably due to the town's prominent Advent Church. Having practiced law and the ministry, Berrick then entered upon a medical career. He attended a series of courses at Hahnemann Medical College in Chicago in 1871 and came back to Buchanan to open a homeopathic medical practice. Dr. Berrick also enjoyed a political career, serving in the state senate and as president of Buchanan. He died in Buchanan on February 9, 1897.

Dr. Francis H. Berrick *(Courtesy Buchanan District Library).*

DR. F. H. BERRICK'S RESIDENCE.

The Dr. Francis H. Berrick home, originally the Lorenzo P. Alexander House, on the northwest corner of West Front and West streets (now 103 Moccasin Street). Berrick bought the magnificent Italianate house in 1885. Alexander, a lumber dealer and contractor, built the house in 1865 and lived there until 1873 when he sold it for the then-stupendous sum of $6,500. *(Courtesy Buchanan District Library)*

A residential street scene in Buchanan, ca. 1910. The unpaved streets are deep in a sticky mire of mud and horse manure. *(Courtesy Buchanan District Library)*

The Clifton O. Hamilton house appears to be a simplified interpretation of the Greek Revival style. Clifton and his wife, Ida, lived on the west side of Buchanan near the corner of Terre Coupe and West Front streets. He inherited the house from his father, Warner O. Hamilton, a farmer, who probably built it about 1865. *(Courtesy Buchanan District Library)*

Stylish homes along one of Buchanan's tree-lined streets. *(Courtesy Buchanan District Library)*

The Lillie Clark house exhibits some Italianate influences with its prominent bay window. *(Courtesy Buchanan District Library)*

The Eli J. and Susan Roe house on Fourth Street, ca. 1910. Eli, a native of the Hoosier State, moved to Buchanan in 1854 and became a successful sawmill owner. He at one time owned and operated seven sawmills, and cut all the timber for the St. Joseph Valley Railroad. He died in Buchanan in 1894. *(Courtesy Buchanan District Library)*

The Matt Kelling house. *(Courtesy Buchanan District Library)*

A winter scene along North Fourth Street, ca. 1910. *(Courtesy Buchanan District Library)*

A magnificent example of the Italianate style with cornice brackets and a nearly flat roof, the Phoebe Broceus house has had a new (and architecturally-incorrect) porch grafted on. Broceus, a widow, lived in this house in town after the death of her husband, William. *(Courtesy Buchanan District Library)*

The original Eli Roe house, ca. 1910. *(Courtesy Buchanan District Library)*

The Levi L. and Mariette Redden home at 113 W. Front Street was built about 1890 and razed after a fire in 1970. The Stick style house incorporated a flamboyant mixture of elements, from the grand porches to the second floor bay window and the eyebrow window on the roof. The Redden House would have qualified as an elegant home in any American city. Unfortunately, the prosperous partner in the grocery firm of Treat & Redden did not enjoy his home for long: he died of "malarial fever" on July 16, 1897, at age 59.*(Courtesy Buchanan District Library)*

The Jacob J. and Emma E. Van Riper house, ca. 1875. The house stood on the southwest corner of Chicago and Clark streets, and the view was taken looking west. Buchanan's Union School, "Fort Sumter," appears in the background. Jacob Van Riper himself stands near the front gate by the little boy riding a rocking horse. The family has dressed in their "Sunday best" and pulled out all their finery for the photographer, including the parlor chairs on the portico floor and roof and the horse and carriage on Chicago Street.

Jacob Van Riper was born in Haverstraw, New York, in 1838, the son of a woolens manufacturer who set up shop in Cass County, Michigan, in 1856. Jacob read law under James M. Spencer of Dowagiac, attended the University of Michigan's law department, and was admitted to the bar in Cassopolis in 1863. Van Riper moved to Buchanan in 1872, relocated from there to Niles in 1887, and finally moved to Berrien Springs in 1893. It was during his time in Buchanan that he served as the attorney general of Michigan (1880-1884). *(Courtesy Buchanan District Library)*

Jacob J. Van Riper (*History of Berrien and Van Buren Counties, Michigan,* 1880)

West Front Street looking east toward town, ca. 1910. Many of Buchanan's social elite lived along this section of the street. *(Courtesy Buchanan District Library)*

A view of West Front Street, ca. 1915. *(Courtesy Buchanan District Library)*

The Clyde Baker House at 313 West Front Street buried in snow, October 10, 1906. A huge snowfall that day virtually paralyzed Berrien County. *(Courtesy Buchanan District Library)*

Claude Roe mowing his lawn, ca 1920. *(Courtesy Buchanan District Library)*

Houses along Clark Street, ca. 1905. *(Courtesy Dale E. Florey Collection)*

The Queen Anne-style Amos C. House residence on the southwest corner of Oak and Front streets. House came to Bertrand Township from his native Pennsylvania in 1865 and built his Buchanan home in 1893. *(Dale E. Florey Collection)*

An unidentified Craftsman-style house in Buchanan, ca. 1910. *(Courtesy Buchanan District Library)*

The William House home on Prairie. Bill House is in the wagon with the dog that hauled him to school. *(Courtesy Buchanan District Library)*

A simple yet elegant frame house in Buchanan, ca. 1910. *(Courtesy Buchanan Preservation Society)*

The Clear Lake Woods Hotel, ca. 1930, was probably one of a series of farmhouses-turned-country hotels that catered to summer tourists eager to escape the city heat. *(Courtesy Buchanan Preservation Society)*

Chapter 6
Transportation

Buchanan's economic base relied on manufacturing and transportation. The town's excellent transportation network opened it to markets and materials from all over the nation. This diverse transportation grid included roads, railroads and steamboats, all of which helped Buchanan grow and prosper.

The Chicago Road served as Buchanan's main highway. During the centuries before Buchanan's birth, Indians had worn a road across southern Michigan to get from southern Lake Michigan to Lake Erie. Michigan's early settlers knew the path as the Great Sauk Trail. The Sauk lived in present-day Illinois and Wisconsin, not Michigan, but they traveled on the road from their homes to the British post of Fort Malden (located in Ontario at Amherstburg, near the mouth of the Detroit River), to collect annuity payments The Sauk Trail, which became the Chicago Road, was a heavily traveled thoroughfare that brought thousands of immigrants into southwest Michigan. Father Gabriel Richard of Detroit, one of Michigan Territory's delegates to Congress, advocated construction of the Chicago Road, and in 1825 introduced a bill to appropriate $1,500 for the survey of a military road between Detroit and Fort Dearborn. Congress generously appropriated $3,000 and surveying began later that year in Detroit. In 1830, President Andrew Jackson signed a bill that appropriated an additional $8,000 for the road's construction.

The road was initially planned to follow a straight east-west route across the state, but the surveyors soon ran into swampland. Realizing that the Indians knew a thing or two about traveling through Michigan, the surveyors wisely abandoned the direct route and instead laid out the Chicago Road along the path of the Great Sauk Trail. Despite the survey, the government made few improvements to the road before 1830, but by 1832 a stagecoach line was running from Detroit to Niles; the line was extended to Chicago the following year.

The second major highway into Berrien County was the Territorial Road, so called because it was provided for by Michigan's territorial council. The Territorial Road branched off from the Chicago Road at Ypsilanti, and then ran through the second tier of counties to St. Joseph. A stagecoach line connected Detroit and St. Joseph by 1834; travelers could catch steamships for Chicago at St. Joseph and thereby complete the entire trip from Detroit to Chicago in five days.

But if the Chicago Road and the Territorial Road looked good on maps, travelers experienced a different reality. Noted British author Harriet Martineau wrote of an 1836 journey on the Chicago Road that, "Juggernaut's car would have been 'broke to bits' on such a road," and that was even before she reached Ypsilanti. Beyond Jonesville in Hillsdale County the road grew worse than ever, until at times everyone had to dismount and walk, and then "such hopping and jumping, such slipping and sliding; such looks of despair from the middle of a pond; such shifting of logs, and carrying of planks, and handing along the fallen trunks of trees." The Territorial Road was apparently in even worse shape than the Chicago Road; when Martineau set off on the return trip to Detroit, she found that rains had rendered the "upper road" completely impassable, and was forced to make the trip by way of the Great Lakes.

The Chicago Road served as a major east-west highway across Michigan for over a century. Later diverted south of Buchanan, the Chicago Road (now US 12) is still an important thoroughfare, although the Indiana Toll Road and Interstate 94 have eclipsed it in importance. The Toll Road, running east-west across extreme northern Indiana and just a few miles south of Buchanan, was completed in 1956. Interstate 94, built as part of the interstate highway system created by the Federal-Aid Highway Act of 1956, opened in sections during the early 1960s and was officially completed from New Buffalo to Port

Huron on February 1, 1967. These two highways removed most of the automobile and truck traffic from Buchanan.

Water transportation also played an important part in Buchanan's early history. Early settlers in Berrien County discovered that keelboats and steamboats could navigate the St. Joseph River for a distance of about 150 miles from its mouth – all the way from St. Joseph to Constantine.

Arks, keelboats and steamboats all appeared on the river in the early 1830s. Arks were essentially rectangular flatboats, built upstream and destined for a one-way trip. Crewmen loaded the ark with freight – usually barrels of flour – and guided them down the river to St. Joseph. There they loaded the flour onto lake ships and tore the arks apart to sell as lumber. Keelboats were vessels built for long-term service. By 1833, about ten or eleven keelboats were already running up and down the river between St. Joseph and Three Rivers. They sailed downstream with the current, unloaded their cargoes, and then headed back upstream propelled by the strong arms and backs of their polemen. The larger keelboats measured eighty feet in length with a seven-foot beam, and carried 350 barrels of flour. After the debut of steamboats, the keelboats usually returned upriver under tow.

Steamboats also served the Buchanan area. Both sidewheelers and sternwheelers operated on the river, including the *Newberryport, Matilda Barney, Davy Crockett, Union, Michawaka, Kalamazoo,* and a dozen or so others. The federal government hired workmen to clear the river of snags and boulders, making the St. Joseph one of Michigan's most important commercial waterways. The arrival of the railroad in Buchanan, Niles and South Bend greatly diminished the importance of river commerce in the upper reaches of the St. Joseph, however, and river traffic there slowly died away. After about 1870, few steamboats attempted to ascend the river as far as Buchanan. This decline came about partly because the railroads monopolized the freight trade and also because the river had become progressively shallower from silt due to farm runoff. By the 1880s, even shallow-draft riverboats could seldom reach Buchanan.

Despite the importance of the St. Joseph River and the Chicago Road, Buchanan might have languished as an isolated backwater village had not the Michigan Central Railroad run its tracks into town in 1849. The Michigan Central linked Detroit with Chicago in 1852 and ranked as one of America's most important railroads. Towns on the Michigan Central, including Ann Arbor, Jackson, Battle Creek, Kalamazoo, Dowagiac and Niles, connected with big city markets. Factories in towns along the Michigan Central could import raw materials and parts and ship out finished goods. Waterpower and the railroad ensured that Buchanan would become a manufacturing center.

The Michigan Central reached Niles on October 2, 1848, to the unrestrained joy of the town's residents. In an age when abominable, muddy roads offered the only alternative to long shipboard voyages, railroads bordered on the miraculous. People could travel quickly on trains, and farmers and manufacturers could ship produce and goods more cheaply. As one Niles businessman declared ecstatically in 1848, "Real estate has advanced about one half in value – our population has increased in about the same proportion. Flour is worth as much here as in Buffalo! Oats, Corn, Butter, Eggs, and in fact almost everything eatable, have bro't from 50 to 100 per cent more than they would if the Road had not come."

The Michigan Central originated with a statewide public improvements project. Michigan's Internal Improvements Act of March 20, 1837, authorized a survey for three railroad lines across the state: the Michigan Northern, Michigan Central and Michigan Southern Railroads. The Michigan Northern would run from St. Clair to the mouth of the Grand River; the Michigan Central from Detroit to St. Joseph; and the Michigan Southern from Monroe to New Buffalo. The state legislature empowered Gov. Stevens T. Mason to borrow five million dollars for the work.

Unfortunately, the Panic of 1837 struck immediately afterward. The national economic depression that followed made railroad financing difficult. The state bought the assets of the Detroit & St. Joseph Railroad, which had begun work on the proposed Michigan Central route, and by February 1838 the line had reached Ypsilanti from Detroit. Work progressed slowly on that line and the Michigan Southern over the next several years, but construction never started on the Michigan Northern. In early 1846, the Michigan Central reached Kalamazoo. Later that year, the state sold both the Michigan Central and Michigan Southern to private owners.

The owners of both railroads realized that the lines' future depended on reaching the rapidly growing city of Chicago. Instead of continuing the Michigan Central's route to St. Joseph, the line dipped south to Dowagiac and Niles, then proceeded west around Lake Michigan to the Windy City. The Michigan Central bridged the St. Joseph River at Niles during the winter of 1848-1849, reached New Buffalo on April 23, 1849, and was completed to Chicago in 1852.

The Michigan Central was an enormous boon to the entire southern tier of Michigan counties. Farmers and manufacturers in Buchanan and elsewhere could easily reach markets in both Chicago and the east coast. The Michigan Central itself became a major source of income for area residents through its purchases of wood. Sawmill workers turned out untold thousands of oak ties, nine feet long and six inches wide, for which the railroad paid twelve and one-half cents each. The locomotives at that time burned wood, so the Michigan Central bought four-foot lengths of cordwood to fuel the railroad engines.

From the beginning, the Michigan Central was an enormously profitable railroad. In 1871, it purchased the newly opened Michigan Air Line Railroad, which had run a track from Niles to Jackson, Michigan. The Michigan Central further expanded its Berrien County operations in 1905 with the lease of the Indiana, Illinois and Iowa Railroad. The I, I & I operated a line from South Bend through Galien, Glendora, Baroda, Derby and Vineland to St. Joseph. This lease gave the Michigan Central a direct link to the port of St. Joseph. In 1904 and 1905, the company double-tracked the entire right-of-way across Michigan so that trains could travel back and forth non-stop instead of waiting on sidings for another train to pass. At its peak popularity in 1920, the Michigan Central ran eighteen daily passenger trains each way between Detroit and Chicago.

Buchanan's second rail line, the St. Joseph Valley Railroad, originated as a narrow-gauge railroad that linked Buchanan with Berrien Springs. Construction on the line began on July 19, 1880, when eight elderly pioneer residents of Buchanan and Berrien Springs broke ground in Buchanan for the roadbed. Farmers and businessmen in the two towns had bought stock in the railroad to fund the work, some of them buying up to five shares at one hundred dollars each. Despite their generosity, the company's limited capital necessitated construction of a narrow gauge track instead of standard gauge; in this case, the track measured three feet between the rails instead of the standard four feet, eight and one-half inches. Grading the roadbed and laying track continued through the fall and spring of 1881.

At its official opening on September 5, 1881, the line ran from the Michigan Central tracks at the south edge of Buchanan up Portage Street (now Red Bud Trail), and then followed the west bank of the St. Joseph River to Berrien Springs. The railroad's rolling stock included a new locomotive purchased from the H. K. Porter Company, three flatcars and a passenger car. Although its owners planned to extend the tracks from Berrien Springs to St. Joseph, they never had the capital to do so. The failure to extend the line northward doomed the St. Joseph Valley. Michigan railroads during the 1880s earned, on average, sixty-eight percent of their revenue from freight traffic. In contrast, freight revenues provided less than half the St. Joseph Valley's total income. The line bought another locomotive and more freight cars, but ridership dropped and losses soared. In September 1886, the St. Joseph Valley went into receivership.

Jonas J. Burns, a railroad entrepreneur from Goshen, Indiana, bought the St.

Joseph Valley in 1889 (renaming it the St. Joseph Valley Railway) and converted it into a standard gauge road. Pledges of money to extend the line to St. Joseph fell through, and in 1893 it closed again. Buchanan finally realized its ambition of a north-south rail connection with St. Joseph and Benton Harbor when the old St. Joseph Valley consolidated with the Benton Harbor and Southeastern Railway Company to form the Milwaukee, Benton Harbor & Columbus Railway. The Pere Marquette Railroad bought the line in 1903 and operated it (usually at a loss) until 1922, when it closed forever.

The major transportation systems gradually bypassed Buchanan. Long-distance automobile traffic left the Chicago Road route after the freeways opened in the 1950s and 1960s. The growing popularity of the automobile cut into rail service, and like other railroads across the country the old Michigan Central saw its business slowly but steadily declining. The South Bend to Baroda tracks were taken up in 1943, and the Glendora to St. Joseph section closed in 1958. In 1930, the New York Central Railroad leased the Michigan Central for a term of ninety-nine years. The New York Central removed one of its two tracks after World War II, leaving only a single set of rails. Passenger service in Buchanan ended, and about 1970 the Buchanan depot was razed. Conrail is now the principle owner of the Michigan Central, with portions of the roadbed owned by Amtrak. Amtrak operates between eight and ten passenger trains each day along the old Detroit to Chicago route, but Niles is the closest passenger stop to Buchanan.

Despite the decline in the city's transportation system, residents and tourists have no trouble reaching Buchanan. The US 31 Bypass (officially the St. Joseph Valley Parkway), completed in the 1990s, provides freeway access just a few miles east of town. US 12 is still an important east-west corridor across Michigan, and the Indiana Toll Road and I-94 also offer major highway connections within a few miles of the city. South Bend Regional Airport also provides airline service to destinations throughout America.

The St. Joseph River. The colonial French first called it the "River of the Miamis" for the Miami Indians who lived along it in the 17th century. By the mid-18th century they referred to it instead as the "River St. Joseph," honoring the patron saint of New France. *(Courtesy Buchanan District Library)*

The St. Joseph River near Buchanan, ca. 1890. The river's scenic beauty began to attract tourists from Chicago as early as the 1880s. Numerous resorts sprang up along the river to cater to these out-of-town guests.

Andrew J. Carothers, a long-time hotel manager in Buchanan, built the river steamer *Nettie June* in 1884. While commercial steamers like the *May Graham* carried passengers and freight, the *Nettie June* was designed for short pleasure trips on the scenic river.

Near the end of the 19th century, Fred Gawthrop offered excursions from Buchanan aboard an oddly-shaped little scow that he christened the *Rudder Grange.* Groups of six to fifteen people could charter the *Rudder Grange,* complete with Gawthorp's guide services, and float downstream to Berrien Springs, Oxbow Bend or all the way to St. Joseph. After reaching their destination they would return via wagon, railroad or the riverboat *May Graham.* Prices ranged from $1.00 to $5.00 per person, depending on the length of the trip and number of excursionists. *(Courtesy Buchanan District Library)*

In mid-August 1898, a group of Buchananites and visitors sailed hilariously down the St. Joseph River from Buchanan to Berrien Springs. They stopped en route at Bear Cave (then known as Scotchtown Cave) and returned home that night on the Milwaukee, Benton Harbor & Columbus Railway. The *Berrien County Record* chronicled their adventures: "Wednesday morning a merry crowd of thirteen, consisting of Mr. and Mrs. Kent, Mr. Graham of Union City, Mrs. Dr. Roe of Chicago, Mr. and Mrs. E. S. Roe, Mr. and Mrs. Charles Pears, Miss Mabelle Roe of Austin, Ill., Mr. and Mrs. George Richards, Dr. Curtis, and Mrs. Nellie Fast, floated down the St. Joe river from Buchanan to Berrien on the boat "Rudder Grange." One of the ladies began the day's festivities by

taking aim at a log lying in the river, but to her dismay it proved a dismal failure for there was no load in the gun. A visit was paid to Scotchtown Cave and several kodak [*sic*] pictures of the crowd were taken with the cave and falls in the background. Dinner was served just across the river from this romantic spot. A gum chewing contest was one of the features of the day, much to the discomfiture of one of the aforesaid gentlemen whose spotless linen suit suffered much in consequence. At rifle practice Charles Pears and Mrs. E. S. Roe carried off the honors, and would have taken the prize, if there had been any, but Dr. Curtis had swallowed it. Berrien was reached about seven o'clock when to sweet strains of music by a street band the party went up to the Hotel de Field [DeField House] where supper awaited them. After supper echoes from the Ladies' Minstrel Show were given in the hotel parlor. The return home was made via the M. B. H. C. R. R."

The *Rudder Grange* measured 24 feet long and six feet wide. Her canvas canopy protected passengers from sun and rain. Amenities included an ice chest, gasoline stove, cooking utensils, dishes and folding tables. *(Courtesy Buchanan District Library)*

A scenic view of the St. Joseph River, ca. 1910. The river's natural beauty attracted visitors from all over the Midwest. Although steamboats served Buchanan into the 1880s railroads were far more important to the town's transportation system. *(Courtesy Buchanan District Library)*

The riverboat *May Graham,* seen near Buchanan ca. 1905, carried passengers and freight on the St. Joseph River from 1879 until 1908. Steamboats tied Buchanan to St. Joseph and points upstream by 1831. Farm runoff and the draining of wetlands lowered the river until by the 1880s steamers could seldom reach Buchanan. On rare occasions the *May Graham* managed to ascend ascend the river to Buchanan. *(Courtesy Buchanan District Library)*

Michigan Central Railroad depot. The Michigan Central reached Buchanan in 1849 and linked Detroit with Chicago three years later. It ranked as one of America's most important rail lines. Most Michigan Central depots, like Buchanan's, were of brick construction. Passengers could also board trains here for the Pere Marquette line that ran from Buchanan to Benton Harbor. *Courtesy Buchanan District Library)*

Five young men pose on a Michigan Central Railroad baggage cart at the Buchanan depot, ca. 1905. Left to right: Frank Stevens, Rollo Bates, Dan Merson, Archie Raven (with bag) and Kern Diggins. *(Courtesy Buchanan District Library)*

Busy day at the Buchanan depot, 1897. Grain elevators stand in the background. Farmers had a contentious relationship with the Michigan Central Railroad, for the it had a near monopoly on shipping grain and other farm products to market. The Patrons of Husbandry (Grange) arose in part as an effort to secure better terms from railroads. Grain elevators, which the farmers themselves often built cooperatively, allowed the farmers to store their grain until commodity prices rose. *(Dale E. Florey Collection)*

A pastoral scene along the Michigan Central Railroad tracks near Buchanan. *(Courtesy Buchanan District Library)*

Ira Wagner (right) helping unload lumber from a Michigan Central Railroad boxcar. The Advent Christian Church appears in the background. *Courtesy Buchanan District Library)*

Frederick McOmber of
Berrien Springs, the
general manager of the St.
Joseph Valley Railway.
(BCHA Collections)

The locomotive "J. J. Burns" of the St. Joseph Valley Railway, ca. 1889. The engine got
its name from railroad owner Jonas J. Burns of Goshen, Indiana. Buchanan businessmen and farmers invested thousands of dollars in this railroad, only to lose it all when
the line went bankrupt in 1893. *(BCHA Collections)*

A Milwaukee, Benton Harbor & Columbus Railway train rounds a curve just north of Buchanan, ca. 1900. The twisting roadbed between Buchanan and Berrien Springs prompted local wags to insist that the railroad's initials, M. B. H. & C., stood for "Many Bumps, Humps and Crooks." *(Courtesy Buchanan District Library)*

Michigan Central train wreck east of the Buchanan depot, ca. 1905. Improved brakes, couplers and other safety equipment made rail travel less hazardous as time went on, but collisions and derailments still took a heavy toll of passengers and crewmen every year. In 1900 alone, accidents killed over 2,500 railroad workers. *(Courtesy Buchanan District Library)*

Railroad accident by the Lee & Porter Company factory. The Lee & Porter Axle Company built its own rail line, the Buchanan & St. Joseph River Railroad, in 1894. This 1.75-mile spur ran from the Michigan Central Railroad depot on the south side of town to the Lee & Porter factory. The Michigan Central bought the line in 1901. It served the Clark Equipment Company factory into the 1970s. *(Courtesy Buchanan District Library)*

Train wreck at the
Lee & Porter Axle
Company, ca. 1900.
A house has come
out on the losing
end of the collision.
*(Courtesy
Buchanan District
Library)*

A train barrels through Buchanan, ca. 1940. *(Courtesy Buchanan District Library)*

Cut through Moccasin Hill, ca. 1900. This road became Red Bud Trail and provided travelers with a route northward to Berrien Springs. *(Courtesy Buchanan District Library)*

Ed Covell drives an omnibus filled with passengers to South Bend, Indiana, 189?. *(Courtesy Buchanan District Library)*

Mr. and Mrs. Fred Andrews in a two-wheeled wagon. Andrews owned a large farm on the southwest side of Buchanan. *(Courtesy Buchanan District Library)*

Dr. C. B. Roe in a buggy, ca. 1890. *(Courtesy Buchanan District Library)*

Francis "Frank" Merson relaxes in a two-seat buggy, ca. 1890. Merson, a livestock dealer, had immigrated to America from England in the 1880s and settled in Buchanan. *(Courtesy Buchanan District Library)*

Buchanan insurance agent William A. Palmer ready for a ride in his cutter, ca. 1890. Even Palmer's heavy coat, boots and cap could not fully insulate against the cold, and long sleigh rides could be miserable ordeals. People often heated a block of soapstone and wrapped it in a towel as a footwarmer. *(Courtesy Buchanan District Library)*

Highway bridge over the St. Joseph River outside Buchanan, ca. 1900. A large sign threatens a $25 fine for anyone cross the bridge "faster than a walk." Construction of this bridge, which replaced a wooden span, began on December 1, 1894. It opened on March 1, 1895. *(Courtesy Buchanan District Library)*

A horse and buggy head out on the scenic drive to Clear Lake, ca. 1900. The route is probably along present-day East Clear Lake Road. *(Courtesy Buchanan District Library)*

Highway bridge over the St. Joseph River on the Niles-Buchanan Road. This steel bridge consisted of two 204-foot spans and a roadway 18 feet wide. *(Courtesy Buchanan District Library)*

An outing in a stylish buggy, ca. 1890. Elina Glover Stephens and George Merrill in the front seat, with Georgia Stephens Halroyd and Mrs. Lammerson Merrill in back. *(Courtesy Buchanan District Library)*

Pete Fuller's omnibus service to Clear Lake, ca. 1890. *(Courtesy Buchanan District Library)*

An elegant carriage in downtown Buchanan, ca. 1890. *(Courtesy Buchanan District Library)*

The Hotel Earl in downtown Buchanan with an omnibus parked in front. Hotels like the Earl ran omnibuses (later shortened to the modern word *bus*) to carry passengers and their luggage from the railroad depot to their door. *(Courtesy Buchanan District Library)*

Charles Mable poses with a new buggy, ca. 1900. Most early automobiles were essentially motorized buggies. *(Courtesy Buchanan District Library)*

A delivery wagon paused in front of the John H. Wynn home, ca. 1890. *(Courtesy Buchanan District Library)*

America experienced a bicycling craze in the 1890s and early 1900s. The invention of the chain drive did away with the old "penny farthing" bicycles that perched the rider atop a huge wheel in front. The picturesque penny farthings were dangerous contraptions that often pitched their riders over the handlebars. The new style of bicycle with two wheels of the same size allowed even women, like these members of the Royal family, to enjoy bicycle rides. *(Courtesy Buchanan District Library)*

Arlin Burns Clark, a young Buchanan machinist, with his bicycle, ca. 1900. Note the large tires that helped negotiate the dirt roads. *(Courtesy Buchanan District Library)*

Clarence Dunbar on one of the Berrien County Sheriff Department's two cylinder Harley Davidson motorcycles. Motorcycles offered speed and economy to law enforcement officers. Motorcycle enthusiasts engaged in hot arguments over the merits of America's two premier brands: Harley Davidson and Indian. *(Courtesy Buchanan District Library)*

Myron S. Mead's 1904 Maxwell. The Maxwell automobile became famous with comedic sketches on Jack Benny's radio show. Benny supposedly drove an ancient Maxwell because he was too stingy to buy a newer car. Jonathan D. Maxwell of Indiana founded a company to build the cars that bore his name in 1903. His firm's first product, the Maxwell Runabout, debuted in 1904 and cost about $500. Myron Mead also bought one of two automobiles produced in Buchanan by the Michigan Motor and Machine Company, which moved to town from Detroit in 1904. Will House bought the one other auto it built before it closed. *(Courtesy Buchanan District Library)*

Adam Lyddick cranks the starter on his automobile. In the days before electric starters, drivers had to hand-crank the engine to start it. Drivers risked broken arms if they held the crank the wrong way and the engine backfired. *(Courtesy Buchanan District Library)*

Buchanan insurance agent William A. Palmer and his daughter Grace prepare for a drive in their Buick, ca. 1910. Like most early automobiles owners, Palmer also kept a horse as a more reliable means of transportation. David Dunbar Buick and his engineer, Walter L. Marr, began building automobiles between 1899 and 1900, and incorporated the Buick Company in 1903. The company became the foundation of General Motors. *(Courtesy Buchanan District Library)*

Charles Landis (standing beside the automobile) and friends return from a successful rabbit hunting expedition, 1913. *(Courtesy Buchanan District Library)*

The Buchanan bridge over the St. Joseph River, photographed on October 21, 1914. Lightly built bridges like this one, built for horse-drawn wagons and carriages, became obsolete with the advent of heavier automobiles and trucks. *(Courtesy Buchanan District Library)*

Herb Bick and Kenneth Mittau after rolling their automobile on the first curve past the railroad tracks on the road to South Bend, ca. 1910. Such accidents were commonplace but, given the low speed of early automobiles, rarely fatal. *(Courtesy Buchanan District Library)*

Charles and Will Lyddick with Guy Young and an early automobile. *(Courtesy Buchanan District Library)*

Buchanan native Virgil Exner (in the driver's seat) transformed the styling of American automobiles with his famous tail fins. *(Courtesy Dale E. Florey Collection)*

Sometimes the fun was just in getting there. Clayton McCollum, Markus Treat and Jack Burk enjoy a winter ride in a one-sheep open sleigh. *(Courtesy Buchanan District Library)*

Chapter 7
Industries

"Every town needs a reason to exist," declared Richard R. Lingemann in his book *Small Town America*. Buchanan's *raison d'existence:* industry.

During its earliest years, Buchanan's industry focused on milling operations. The first industrial production in Berrien County began in the Buchanan area when Isaac McCoy set up a horse-powered gristmill at the Carey Mission in about 1826. Aside from this early small-scale industrial effort, Buchanan's manufacturing base originated because of McCoy's Creek. The creek rises in Buchanan Township and descends in a northeasterly direction until it empties into the St. Joseph River. Early settlers immediately realized that they could harness the creek's waterpower to run mills and factories. Over the years, at least thirteen different mills sprang up along McCoy's Creek to grind flour, cut lumber or power machinery.

Charles Cowles built the first of these mills in 1833 soon after he arrived from Vermont. His shingle mill operated for about a year until he sold it to Dr. Charles C. Wallin, who converted it into a gristmill to produce cornmeal and graham flour. Other early mills included a sawmill built by Russell McCoy and the Hatfield and Atkins sawmill, both built in 1835; the Day and Hamilton gristmill (1839); and a wool-carding mill (ca. 1845). The Bainton Niagara Mill numbered among the town's most famous milling operations. Built sometime around 1880, the mill turned out excellent flour marketed under the brand name of "Niagara." A fire in 1924 destroyed the Niagara Mill, and it was never rebuilt.

Of all Buchanan's mills, only the Pears Mill survives into the twenty-first century. William H. Bainton, a miller from England, had immigrated to America around 1856 and settled in Buchanan. He entered into partnership with William Beach and built a three-story gristmill in 1857. William Pears, a farmer and fellow English immigrant, soon joined Bainton and was in charge of the milling operations at the time Bainton died in 1865. Pears then went into partnership with one or more of the Rough brothers, a family of prosperous farmers from Portage Prairie, and the milling operation became Rough and Pears. William Pears' son, Charles, took over the day-to-day operations of the mill after William died in 1893. The economic depression that plagued agriculture throughout the 1920s climaxed in the stock market collapse of 1929 and the onset of the Great Depression of the 1930s. Charles Pears lost the mill about 1933 as the economy hit its nadir, but Buchanan Co-ops, Inc., assumed ownership and kept it operating for the next fifty years. During that time, Buchanan Co-ops removed the mill's third story and covered the building exterior with sheet metal.

When the old Pears Mill closed in 1983, many people assumed that Buchanan's last extant mill building would be razed. Fortunately for area history, the Buchanan Preservation Society stepped in and restored the building as a museum and operating gristmill. Wooden clapboard replaced the metal siding and millstones once more ground grain into flour. The Preservation Society operates the mill during summer months and plans to restore its third floor to return the building to its original 1850s appearance.

Although Buchanan's industrial base originated with mills, other manufacturing flourished during the mid-nineteenth century. Factories in the town took advantage of Buchanan's proximity to natural resources (particularly the hardwood forests), waterpower from McCoy's Creek, and its excellent transportation system with the Michigan Central Railroad and the St. Joseph River. Unlike northern Michigan, with its vast forests of white pine, Berrien County's indigenous woods were composed of oak, maple, beech, walnut and hickory – ideal material for furniture, tool handles and other wood products.

The Rough Brothers Wagon Works took advantage of Buchanan's plentiful supply of lumber to manufacture farm wagons. The business originated in the 1840s, when Jacob Luther opened a wagon-making factory on Days Avenue. Several ownership changes ensued, and in 1872 the business became a joint stock company called the Buchanan Manufacturing Company. People all over Buchanan bought stock in the firm, which erected a massive, four-story brick factory on the east side of North Main Street. Andrew C. Day and Solomon Rough bought the company in 1875, and four years later it came under the ownership of brothers Solomon, William R. and George H. Rough. The company's forty employees built some 1,500 wagons and carriages each year.

Many Michiganders knew of Buchanan as a furniture-manufacturing center. The Black & Willard Furniture Company numbered among the earliest and most prominent of these concerns. Augustine Willard, a young man from Ashburnham, Massachusetts, had started the business in New Buffalo in 1855 and then moved it to Buchanan in 1860, where he set up shop on Oak Street. Horace S. Black and his son Charles S. bought the company in 1865 and ran it until 1872, when Horace took over the entire operation. The business then moved to a factory building known as "Fort Sumter," which was possibly a pun on Horace's middle name: Sumner. Willard, who had worked as the factory foreman, rejoined the firm as a partner in 1875. Black & Willard specialized in making bedsteads, tables, lounges and other fine furniture. The Chicago *Commercial Advertiser* remarked in 1874 that Black's goods "run through many grades from the common styles up. He has many unique and original designs of his own for his finer furniture." Walnut lumber from area forests went into the Black & Willard furniture, and the company sold its products through-out the Midwest and South.

In 1875, Black & Willard moved its operations into the old Floral Hall and Skating Rink building on the northeast side of Buchanan. The Buchanan Park Association had built the two-story octagonal structure in 1869. An Archimedes screw lifted water from McCoy's Creek to flood the floor for ice-skating during the winter; in the summertime, the Floral Hall hosted a fair where area residents exhibited their horticultural and handiwork items. The building apparently did not see long-term use in this civic function, for it appears in an 1873 plat of the village as a washing machine and wringer factory. Horace Black died in 1886, at which time the firm had a value of nearly $20,000. Black & Willard apparently ceased operations around 1900.

Like Black & Willard, the Buchanan Manufacturing Company also used locally-produced lumber for its production. Founded as a stock company in 1872, the firm bought a vacant handle factory near the Michigan Central Railroad line on Oak Street and went into business making furniture. Andrew C. Day served as company president, with William Osborne as secretary and manager. Within two years the factory employed sixty workmen, who turned out $100,000 worth of furniture each year. The company specialized in making a spindle maple bedstead and, like Black & Willard, sold its furniture primarily in the Midwest and South.

John E. Barnes went into partnership with Benajah H. Spencer to form the Spencer Barnes Company in 1874. The firm had started in 1872 as a partnership between Spencer and Jacob Allen, became Spencer & Willard later that year when Allen sold his share of the business to Augustine Willard, and then became Spencer & Barnes after John Barnes succeeded Willard. The new furniture company enjoyed rapid growth and soon needed to secure larger manufacturing facilities. Benton Harbor had then eclipsed the Niles and Buchanan area as a manufacturing center, and Barnes elected to transfer his operations to the former town. The Spencer Barnes Company moved from Buchanan to Benton Harbor in 1891. Although Spencer Barnes had left Buchanan, company president John Barnes wanted to continue manufacturing there. In 1892, he and W. S. Wells and Alfred Richards orga-nized another stock furniture factory, the Buchanan Cabinet Company. By 1905, the company had become the largest factory in Buchanan and employed over one hundred workers. The company closed down its operations in 1918.

Not all of Buchanan's nineteenth century manufacturers based their operations on locally available raw materials. One of largest operations, the Zinc Collar Pad Company, came about as an invention by town resident Dexter Curtis. Curtis, Henry Gilman and George H. Richards founded Zinc Collar Pad in 1870. The firm quickly became one of Buchanan's largest and most famous industries. Originally founded as "Curtis, Gilman & Richards," the business soon adopted the Zinc Collar Pad name. As its title suggested, the company manufactured a horse collar pad made of zinc. Zinc oxide, still the active ingredient in modern medicinal ointments, helps heal skin sores. Curtis took advantage of the metal's natural curative powers to invent a horse collar pad that helped heal the sores that formed where leather collars abraded the animal's skin. The company began production in a factory near the Michigan Central depot, and then moved to a facility on the southwest corner of Chicago and Oak streets after the original factory burned in 1874. Orders for the Zinc Collar Pad poured in and within a few years the company had become one of America's largest consumers of zinc. By 1880, the factory workers turned out 7,000 to 10,000 collar pads per year. Henry Gilman sold his share in the business to Curtis soon after he helped found the company. George Richards' son, Joseph L. Richards, became the firm's general superintendent after his father's death in 1888; in 1894, he bought out Dexter Curtis' two-thirds interest and assumed control of the company. After Joseph died in 1906, his sons Joseph L., Jr., and George H. took over the business. The Zinc Collar Pad Company remained an important part of Buchanan's industrial base for a half century, but the advent of tractors, trucks and automobiles in the early twentieth century diminished the use of carriage and draft horses. Demand for the Zinc Collar Pad dwindled, and in 1925 the company ceased production.

The Hatch Cutlery Company was founded in South Milwaukee, Wisconsin, in 1892. The company vice president and treasurer, W. P. Hatch, had started his business career at age fourteen as an office boy with the Union Knife Company in Connecticut. He worked his way up in the company until he attained the position of general manager, with up to 150 employees under his supervision. Hatch Cutlery formed when Hatch went into partnership with D. P. Eells of Cleveland, Ohio, who came on board as company president. The company moved to Buchanan in 1894, where it bought a large factory building from Rough Brothers and added a foundry. There it produced pocketknives and shears. Unfortunately, Hatch Cutlery did not prosper in Buchanan, possibly due to the Depression of 1893 and the poor business conditions that followed for several years. The firm went into receivership on April 19, 1895, and closed shortly thereafter. Clarence Sprague of Waterville, Connecticut, reopened the plant under the name of the Michigan Cutlery Company. It soon became the Sprague Cutlery Company, went into receivership again, and finally closed in 1898.

The Lee & Porter Company opened in Dowagiac on July 1, 1894 to manufacture carriage and wagon axles and its unique product: the Porter Sandband Axle. Two Dowagiac residents, Fred E. Lee, president of the Round Oak Stove Company, and axle inventor Henry H. Porter had founded the company. Lee, as one of the original stockholders of the Buchanan Power and Electric Company, could claim ten percent of the electric power generated by the Buchanan dam. In October 1894, Lee & Porter moved its production to a new factory beside the Buchanan dam to take advantage of the hydroelectric power. By 1895, the company employed some forty workers. The company shipped its axles to a worldwide market, and made a wire-spoked wheel used on rickshaws in India and China. Lee & Porter pursued the developing automobile market and saw a steady growth for its products, especially a new axle developed by R. J. Burrows. By about 1912, the company's 130 to 150 workers turned out 20 pairs of front and rear automobile axles every day, and the company claimed prominence as Buchanan's largest single employer. The firm even operated its own railroad line, the Buchanan and St. Joseph River Railroad, a 1.75-mile spur that tied into the Michigan Central line on the south side of town. Disaster hit on February 10, 1913, when a fire leveled the Lee & Porter factory. The company lost about $300,000 in machinery and equipment. The American Gear Company of Jackson, Michigan, bought out Lee & Porter's unfilled contracts under an agreement that forbade the latter's reconstruction. Although Lee & Porter disappeared from Buchanan, its demise helped foster development of the Clark Equipment Company. Eugene B. Clark, president of what was then the Celfor Tool Company, persuaded Burrows to leave American Gear and return to Buchanan. Burrows developed an improved truck axle for Celfor, which soon changed its name to Clark Equipment.

Football legend Knute Rockne inspired the name of another Buchanan company: Electro-Voice. In 1927, Al Kahn and Lou Burroughs had formed a partnership in South Bend, Indiana, to service radio receivers. Their business did well, but the Great Depression nearly ruined them. They sold off what remained of their service and retail business to concentrate on the audio field. Notre Dame football coach Knute Rockne bought what might have been the world's first portable public address system from them. Rockne, recovering from an illness, had found it impossible to supervise players on all four of his practice fields. He built a tower that overlooked all the fields, and had Kahn and Burroughs design a PA system with a switching mechanism for it so that he could call out directions to each field. Rockne dubbed the system his "Electric Voice," and the name (slightly altered) stuck. On July 1, 1930, the firm incorporated as Electro-Voice."

Electro-Voice prospered in the audio communications field. The firm paid off all its creditors by 1933, and by 1936 it had twenty employees working for it. When the United States entered World War II in 1941, the federal government restricted the production of civilian goods and Electro-Voice's contracts disappeared. The company concentrated on a noise-canceling microphone that filtered out extraneous sounds. The military finally recognized the microphone's qualities in combat, where it cut the sounds of battle noise so that the human voice came through clearly. The T-45, attached to soldiers' helmets, proved an enormous success. By 1943, the company was turning out 2,500 microphones per day. Electro-Voice won an E-Award for its wartime contributions.

The company moved from South Bend to Buchanan in 1946, immediately after World War II. Electro-Voice returned to the civilian market, manufacturing microphones, public address systems, speakers, phonograph cartridges and other audio products. Electro-Voice products went into space as special microphones for NASA's Skylab space station, equipment that performed flawlessly throughout Skylab's six-year mission. Kahn and Burroughs sold Electro-Voice to Gulton Industries in 1967, which in turn sold it to Mark IV Industries in the mid-1980s. The company became part of Telex, which in 1999 and the early 2000s transferred most of Electro-Voice's operations to its headquarters in suburban Minneapolis.

The early twentieth century saw many of Buchanan's early industries close their doors. As these companies dwindled in number, Buchanan came to rely on Clark Equipment Company as its reason for existence, as noted in the next chapter. Changing corporate dynamics in the late twentieth century, including industrial globalization, new workforce needs and reliance on different forms of transportation, transformed Buchanan. Clark left Buchanan, as did industries in nearby towns (Studebaker in South Bend and Kawneer in Niles, to name but two) that had employed scores of Buchanan workers.

An early photograph of the "Niagara" flour mill in Buchanan. *(BCHA Collections,*

Pears Mill in the background, ca. 1900, as a "Mr. Richardson" brings a prodigious load of logs into town. *(Courtesy Buchanan District Library)*

The natural feature responsible for the creation of Buchanan and its industries: McCoy's Creek. *(Courtesy Buchanan District Library)*

Painters at the Rough Brothers Wagon Works, ca. 1890. These skilled artisans did not merely paint the wooden wagons, but pinstriped them in bright colors. *(Courtesy Buchanan District Library)*

The Rough Brothers Wagon Works, ca. 1880. *(Courtesy Buchanan District Library)*

This huge brick building on North Main Street housed the Rough Brothers Wagon Works. The crack in the photograph comes from a break in the glass plate negative. *(Courtesy Buchanan District Library)*

The Black & Willard Furniture Company on the east edge of Buchanan, 1875. The factory occupied the Floral Hall and Skating Rink building, constructed in 1869, which featured an unusual octagonal structure measuring seventy feet in diameter. The octagon appears in the center of this photograph, covered by its nearly circular roof. *(Courtesy Buchanan District Library)*

C. S. Black & Son Furniture Company. *(Courtesy Buchanan District Library)*

Charles S. Black and his wife, Emma. Black was a partner in the Black & Willard Furniture Company. *(Courtesy Buchanan District Library)*

The Zinc Collar Pad Company, ca. 1890. A horse, counterbalanced by the weight of zinc collar pads and probably not happy about the experience, hangs suspended from the wagon thills. *(Courtesy Buchanan District Library)*

The Zinc Collar Pad Company factory on the southwest corner of Chicago and Oak streets, ca. 1890. *(Courtesy Buchanan District Library)*

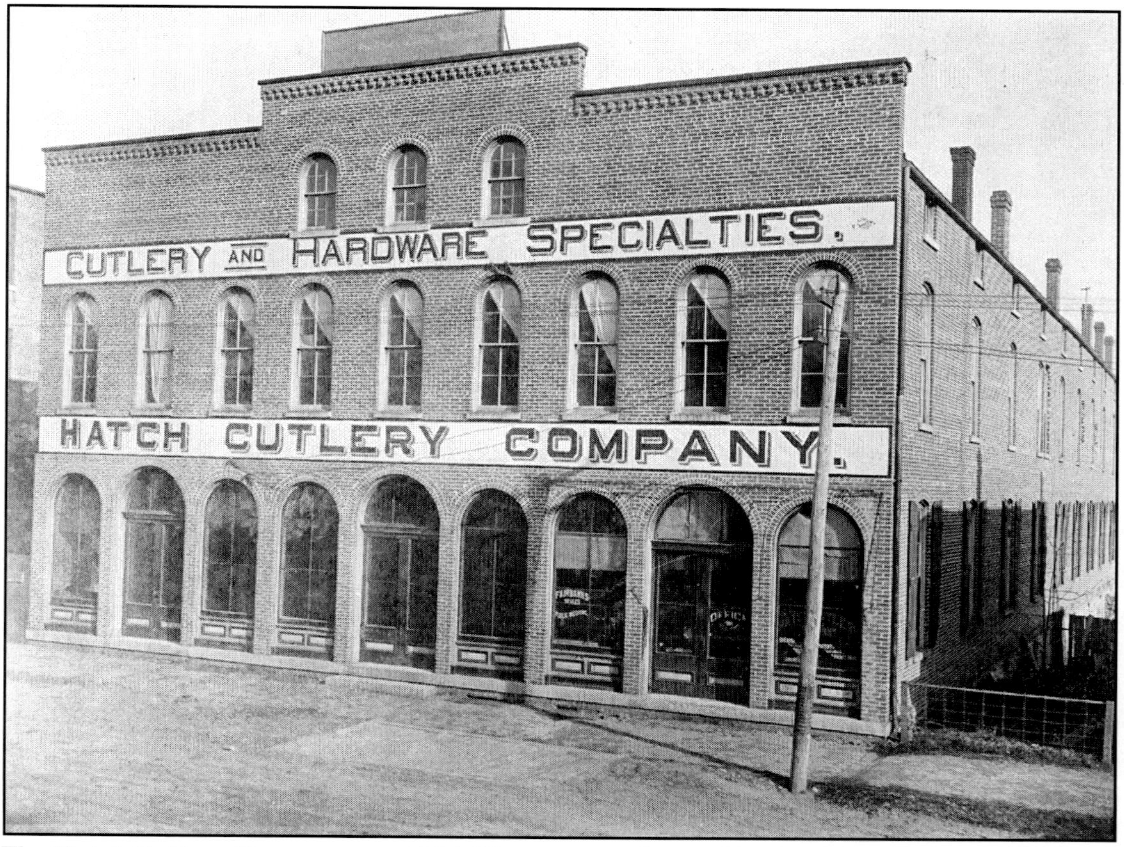

The Hatch Cutlery Company, ca. 1894. The company located in the old Rough Brothers Wagon Works factory on North Main Street. *(Courtesy Buchanan District Library)*

Workers at the Hatch Cutlery Company pose for a photograph, ca. 1895. In the days before child labor laws, boys like those seated in the front row often worked long hours in factories. *(Courtesy Buchanan District Library)*

The workers at a Buchanan furniture factory on Oak Street, ca. 1900. *(Courtesy Buchanan District Library)*

This photograph is entitled simply "Our Tree, 1884." Perhaps a storm blew over a tree in someone's yard, but the huge trunk is almost certainly destined for a local sawmill. Identified from left to right are Messrs. Richerson, Jackson, Hathaway, Helmick, and Myron Mead at his sawmill on Chicago Road. *(Courtesy Buchanan District Library)*

Michigan's forests produced immense quantities of lumber, including these boards drying at the Hopkins Lumber Yard. *(Courtesy Buchanan District Library)*

Hopkins Sawmill, 1927. *(Courtesy Buchanan District Library)*

Eaton Johnson prepares to drive an enormous log off to market, probably to Hopkins Saw-mill, ca. 1900. *(Courtesy Buchanan District Library)*

Workmen at the Blodgett brickyard in Buchanan, 1901. Men are identified as, left to right: John Jarvis, Guy Eisenhart, Ed Conrad, Frank Blodgett, Liberty Dragoo, Fred Fedore, James Matthews, Henry Blodgett and Charles Chatterton. *(Courtesy Buchanan District Library)*

Thousand of bricks dry at the Blodgett Brickyard in Buchanan. The chimney for the kiln where the bricks were baked appears in the right background. The clay bricks had to bake at the right temperature: too low and they would crumble, too high and they would fuse into a glassy material. *(Courtesy Buchanan District Library)*

An early view of the Lee & Porter Axle Company on the northeast edge of Buchanan, ca. 1895. *(Courtesy Buchanan District Library)*

The Lee & Porter Axle Co. factory, ca. 1910. Lee & Porter had its own rail line, the Buchanan & St. Joseph River Railroad, which ran 1.75 miles from the factory to the Michigan Central depot on the south side of town. *(Courtesy Buchanan District Library)*

The Lee & Porter Axle Company, ca. 1910. *(Courtesy Buchanan District Library)*

Workers at the Lee & Porter Axle Company stand proudly in front of a sign proclaiming the company's various products, ca. 1900. *(Courtesy Buchanan District Library)*

Alto Denno beside his workbench in the Lee & Porter Axle Co. factory, ca. 1900. *(Courtesy Buchanan District Library)*

Fire destroyed the Lee & Porter Axle Company on February 10, 1913. The company never rebuilt. *(Courtesy Buchanan District Library)*

The Buchanan Creamery on Portage Street, ca. 1915. Creameries converted highly-perishable milk and cream into butter and cheese. *(Courtesy Buchanan District Library)*

Offices and factory of the Buchanan Cabinet Company, ca. 1900. *(Courtesy Buchanan District Library)*

The Buchanan Cabinet Company produced kitchen cabinets and desks, and was once the town's largest employer of factory workers. The factory stood on the corner of Days Avenue and First Street, and closed in 1918. *(Courtesy Buchanan District Library)*

Buchanan Cabinet Company workers, ca. 1900. *(Courtesy Buchanan District Library)*

Workers in the Buchanan Cabinet Company factory, ca. 1900. They are
identified only by their last names: Cloud, Wood and Glidden. The man at far
right is unknown. *(Courtesy Buchanan District Library)*

The Buchanan Cabinet Company, ca. 1910. Nine of the workmen are identified: Alfred Richards (standing in left doorway wearing light hat); Tom Burks (front row, third from left); Sam Bunker (front row, fourth from left in white shirt); David Schwartz (standing behind and between Sam Bunker and Tom Burks); Mr. Smith (front row, sixth from left); E. E. Glidden (in right doorway, wearing a necktie); George Otto (right side of right doorway, in white shirt); Frank Barnes (to right of George Otto, in dark shirt and suspenders); Fulton O. Powers (front row, third from right). *(BCHA Collections)*

Clam shells from the St. Joseph River. Various factories along the river made buttons for clothing from these freshwater clam shells. *(Courtesy Buchanan District Library)*

Buchanan's Advent Christian Church became an industrial building, the Pattern Worker, after the church congregation disbanded in the 1920s. The old Greek Revival-style church building was demolished in 1957. *(Courtesy Buchanan District Library)*

The Marble Works in Buchanan, run by Joseph P. Beistle and shown here about 1890, made gravestones and worked with granite as well. Note the caskets lying to the right of the shop. The business may also have manufactured stone tabletops for the local furniture factories. *(Courtesy Buchanan District Library)*

A somewhat fanciful artist's depiction of the Campbell Transmission Company. *(Courtesy Buchanan District Library)*

The Campbell Transmission Company incorporated in Buchanan in November 1921 with L. L. Campbell as president and Leon J. Campbell as secretary. The firm built automobile and truck transmissions. It closed about 1926. *(Donald F. Ryman Collection)*

The factory floor at the Campbell Transmission Company. *(Donald F. Ryman Collection)*

Chapter 8
Clark Equipment

The city of Buchanan became synonymous with the Clark Equipment Company. Although not a true "company town" in the fashion of Pullman, Illinois, or Hershey, Pennsylvania, Buchanan's economic and social life revolved around Clark Equipment. Families and their neighbors worked for Clark. People lived in Clark-built houses, played on Clark-sponsored sports teams and enjoyed entertainment at the Clark Theater. The city and Clark grew up together. Clark's departure in the 1980s devastated Buchanan, creating a void that the city has only begun to fill.

Clark originated in Chicago in 1902 as the George R. Rich Manufacturing Company. The firm manufactured a boring bar that George R. Rich, a mechanic and employee of the Illinois Steel Company, had invented. Rich's drill proved superior to anything on the market and sales soared. The company outgrew its Chicago factory and began looking for a factory site that offered room for expansion, a good labor market and a source of cheap electrical power. In the fall of 1904, W. B. Johnson, the firm's new general manager, spotted a newspaper advertisement in which the Business Men's Association of Buchanan offered low rent and low-cost electrical power to any manufacturing company willing to relocate in the village. These factors, plus Buchanan's proximity to Chicago markets, made it a perfect fit for the George R. Rich Company.

The George R. Rich Company moved to Buchanan with about twenty-eight of its employees in November 1904. It occupied a vacant brick factory building that had housed the Hatch Cutlery Company. In exchange for the many inducements that Buchanan offered, Rich promised to remain in Buchanan for at least three years.

Eugene B. Clark, an assistant superintendent of Illinois Steel, came on board as a director of the George R. Rich Company. He toured the Buchanan operation in 1905 with other directors from Illinois Steel and found the operation in a shambles. The company was heavily in debt, with high expenses and low sales. Clark elbowed George Rich out of the company and replaced Johnson with Merton L. Hanlin. Hanlin seemed an odd choice for a corporate executive. His sole managerial experience was reorganizing Illinois Steel's company cafeteria and he had, in fact, always aspired to a career as a comedic entertainer. Clark's assessment of Hanlin's executive abilities, however, proved correct. Hanlin possessed a natural talent for management and, with help from Clark and other Illinois Steel executives, soon had the company on a profitable footing.

Buchanan built a new factory building for the Rich Company on McCoy's Creek, east of Portage Street, in 1906. The company had developed a new type of twist drill made of high-speed steel that could drill deep, clean holes. The company christened it the Celfor Drill, combining the Latin words *celeritas* (rapid or swift) and *fortis* (strong). George Rich's departure from the firm and the new product made a name change in order. On January 1, 1907, the firm became the Celfor Tool Company.

Eugene Clark had left Illinois Steel in August 1906 to take control of the Rich Company. While on a business trip to Europe three years later, he saw industries there producing high-grade steel castings with electric furnaces, a system still unknown in the United States. Clark recommended that Celfor take advantage of local labor and electrical power to create a new steel-producing industry in Buchanan using the electric furnace process. The Buchanan Electric Steel Company was organized in 1910 with Clark as its president.

Clark's role in Buchanan's economic and cultural life mushroomed during the First World War. After war broke out in 1914, the Allies and the United States government placed large orders with Celfor and Buchanan Electric Steel for steel wheels, axles, internal gear drives and other products. The two companies merged in December 1916 in order to raise the necessary capital for expansion. The merger created a new entity: the Clark Equipment Company. The company built new factories and hired more workers.

Clark's growing involvement in the community's cultural scene probably developed out of Merton Hanlin's love of theater and entertainment in general. The Rich Company, with Hanlin's support, had begun sponsoring a baseball team in 1905. Like many company-sponsored ball teams throughout the Midwest, the Clark baseball team featured outstanding athletes who, not coincidentally, happened to work for Clark during the day and play ball on evenings and weekends. Buchanan's village musical band became the Clark Band in 1917. In 1917-1918, Clark Equipment built the 600-seat Clark Theater where, among other activities, the Clark Players staged theatrical plays. When the worldwide Spanish influenza pandemic struck Buchanan in October 1918, killing sixty-four residents of the city and township, Clark set up a temporary hospital in a large house on Rynearson Street. This became the Clark Hospital, which served Buchanan for the next ten years. Many residents even lived in Clark homes. Beginning in 1918, the company-sponsored Buchanan Land Company built houses for employees in the Liberty Heights subdivision.

Clark continued to expand in Buchanan and elsewhere in Michigan during the booming 1920s. The company weathered the postwar economic depression of 1920-1921 without major difficulty. Production facilities expanded in Buchanan. The company opened new factories in Berrien Springs in 1920 and Battle Creek in 1923, and acquired the Frost Gear and Forge Company in Jackson in 1929. The Buchanan factories churned out axles, transmissions, housings and drills, much of it going to supply the nation's growing automobile industry.

The national economy – and Clark's prospects – looked rosy as the 1920s drew to a close. Some aspects of the economy, notably agriculture and mining, had been mired in recession since World War I, but other industries were booming. Clark products went to nearly every automobile and truck manufacturer in the country, and Clark wanted to expand. Clark had funded most of its growth through its own reinvested profits, but in 1929 the firm's directors decided to put its stock on the New York Stock Exchange. Clark stock went on the "Big Board" on October 17, 1929. Twelve days later, on "Black Friday," the stock market crashed. The Great Depression had begun.

Clark's sales and profits spiraled downward as the Depression took effect. Sales dropped from $15.5 million in 1929 to $9 million in 1930 and $2.35 million in 1932; profits plummeted from $1.3 million in 1929 to $327,000 in 1930, and a loss of $802,000 in 1932. The automaker Graham Paige, which had bought 40% of Clark's axles and transmissions, cancelled all its orders. The company had to lay off workers to stem the flow of red ink. Employment at Clark's Buchanan plants had peaked at 1,550 in 1929; by 1933, only 577 employees remained on the job.

Besides layoffs and other cost-cutting measures, Clark developed new products in an attempt to respond to the Depression. In November 1932 it debuted the Autotram, a revolutionary new self-propelled railroad car built at Clark's Battle Creek factory. The Autotram offered the railroad industry a radical departure from the standard system of steam locomotives pulling a string of passenger cars. A sixteen-cylinder Chrysler gasoline engine powered the Autotram, which also featured streamlining, lightweight aluminum construction, and a new style of shock-absorbing trucks. Best of all, the fast Autotram (it hit speeds of over seventy miles per hour) could be operated by a small crew and thereby save labor costs. The Autotram made a big splash with the public at the Chicago World's Fair in 1933, but the ultra-conservative railroad executives remained unimpressed. No orders ever arrived, and Clark finally abandoned the project. Clark recovered some of its $100,000 investment in the Autotram when streetcar and subway car makers bought the trucks designed for the Autotram for their own cars. The Buchanan factory turned out the castings and axles for this new product.

A second Clark innovation during the Depression years was the Clark-Air, an air-conditioned bed. Clark officials hit on the idea of an air-conditioned bed as an attractive energy-saving appliance: instead of cooling their whole house, homeowners could just cool the bed itself. Clark already built air-conditioning units and a private inventor, William L. Morrison, had created just such a bed, so in 1934 Clark provided Morrison with capital and workspace to perfect and manufacture his bed. The product went on the market in 1935 as the Clark-Air. Unfortunately, the Clark-Air found few buyers. It carried a high price tag (a drawback in the Depression years) and its unconventional appearance scared away customers. Clark dropped the program after two independent market studies revealed that only a small market existed for the bed.

Clark's fortunes began to rebound after the Depression bottomed out in 1932. Employment rose, the company raised workers' wages five cents per hour in 1934 and again in 1937, and stock dividends slowly increased. Clark had enjoyed fairly good labor relations, but strikes in automobile factories in Flint and Detroit helped spread worker dissatisfaction to Buchanan. In May 1938, Clark workers voted to unionize with the Reliable Workmen of America (RIW), choosing it over the UAW-CIO or a local company union. Two years later, however, Clark employees voted out the RIW in favor of the UAW-CIO.

Clark began gearing up for war production in the late 1930s as World War II loomed on the horizon. As government orders rolled in, employment at Clark rose to 2,201 workers in 1939. Some departments worked full-time, seven days a week. Clark products like axles, housings, transmissions and industrial lift trucks all had obvious military applications. The federal government determined what companies would receive scarce materials for production, but that posed no challenge to Clark. Clark already sold 60% of its output to truck manufacturers, and the military needed fantastic numbers of trucks. In September 1941, the government gave 95% of Clark's output a preferred defense rating.

Clark went into full war production after Pearl Harbor. Sales rose from a little less than $12.5 million in 1939 to $35.8 million in 1941 and over $77 million in 1943. The Buchanan and Battle Creek factories both won the prestigious Army-Navy "E" Pennant for excellence in production. Clark's biggest production increase came in its "Tructractor" department, which made forklifts and towing machines. Sales of these vehicles rose to 17,000 in 1944 alone and accounted for over half of Clark's total income. Clark even built a miniature bulldozer, the CA-1 that could fit into transport planes and gliders. Clark employees shared in the wartime wealth: factory workers' wages rose from an average of 62 cents per hour in 1937 to $1.13 in 1944.

World War II also changed Buchanan's cultural composition. Scores of Clark employees went into military service just as the company hired workers to meet the sky-rocketing needs of war production. Berrien County perennial labor shortage reached a critical stage by 1943. Between two-thirds and three-fourths of Buchanan's population was engaged in industrial labor, mostly at Clark. Clark's housing, transmission and gear departments worked seven days a week.

Like several Berrien County companies, Clark imported workers from the Deep South to solve its labor crisis. Recruiting agents traveled to southern states, primarily Arkansas, Alabama and Mississippi, bringing in over three thousand workers for Clark alone. Good-paying factory jobs enticed these Southerners, especially the impoverished tenant farmers who had no land or economic ties to the South. For African-Americans, work in the North also offered a route of escape from the South's racist Jim Crow laws. These new employees had no experience in shop work and had to be trained in the shortest time possible.

The enormous influx of factory workers strained Buchanan's housing and utilities systems. Buchanan's population rose from about 4,000 people in 1940 to nearly 6,000 in 1945. Established residents also had to cope with a population whose cultural background was markedly different than its own. The federal government partially resolved the housing crisis by bringing in dozens of trailer units, which it set up in camps segregated by race. The cultural differences between the long-term residents of Buchanan and the recently employed Southern workers were more deep-seated. Southerners had different customs, accents and speech patterns than their neighbors, and the African-Americans faced the added challenges of racism.

The war years also saw changes in Clark's top management. Eugene B. Clark, who had built the corporation from the ground up, died in 1942. Albert S. Bonner, who had joined the company in 1915, succeeded him as company president. Bonner worked hard, drank hard and - according to one associate - ate nothing but steak and chocolate pudding. His unorthodox lifestyle may have taken a toll on his health, for he died suddenly of a heart attack in February 1945. Bonner's death brought George Spatta to the head of Clark. Born in New York City's infamous Hell's Kitchen of immigrant Swiss parents, Spatta never forgot his humble origins. Eugene Clark had hired him away from General Electric, and Spatta brought with him three fundamental rules of success: know your job, work hard, and get along with people. Clark employees liked Spatta, and he built the firm into an international corporation.

Clark reorganized and expanded under Spatta's leadership. The company built a new factory in Jackson and consolidated its transmission manufacturing there in 1948-1949, closing its Berrien Springs plant. In 1949, Clark sold its drill division to the Republic Drill and Tool Company – the company's first major divestiture and the end of the original product brought in by George R. Rich. Clark bought the Ross Carrier Company of Benton Harbor in 1953 and built a new factory there, introducing the company to the manufacture of earth-moving equipment that would become a mainstay of its production. The "Michigan" line of construction machinery, consisting of three models of tractor shovels, began deliveries in 1954, and soon expanded to include scrapers and dozers.

Labor unrest affected Clark's Buchanan operations during the late 1950s and 1960s. Strikes at the Jackson factory and in automobile factories that used Clark products idled workers at the Buchanan plant in 1957. Another strike in Jackson and Battle Creek in 1961 put 700 of Clark's 1,800 Buchanan employees out of work. Workers staged major strikes in Buchanan itself in 1963 and 1965. These strikes cost employees and employers enormous amounts of money in lost wages and production.

Labor problems and international expansion fueled concerns in Buchanan that Clark might leave town entirely. Acquisitions of other companies and construction of new factories meant that Clark had fewer and fewer ties to its home city. Clark bought Brown Trailers, Inc., in 1958 and Tyler Refrigeration in 1963, giving it factories in cities across America. In the late 1950s and early 1960s, Clark bought companies or opened factories in Canada, Europe, Asia, South America, Australia and New Zealand. Companies all over the world built Clark products under license arrangements. This national and international expansion loosened Clark's ties to Buchanan.

Walter E. Schirmer oversaw much of Clark's foreign expansion. He had become the firm's executive vice president and in 1963 succeeded George Spatta as president. Spatta moved up to board chairman. Under Schirmer's leadership, Clark grew into a multinational giant. By 1969, Clark's sales outside of America exceeded all of its sales put together in 1960. Clark products were sold in 156 different countries in 1971, and the company boasted 17 manufacturing subsidiaries and 30 licensees. Schirmer stayed at the helm until 1973, when he became chairman of the board of directors and Bert E. Phillips replaced him as Clark's president.

During the late 1970s, Clark shifted production from Michigan factories to states in the South. In October 1982, Buchanan's worst fears were realized when Clark announced that it would close its Buchanan, Benton Harbor and Jackson manufacturing plants and slash production at its Battle Creek factory. The company cited high manufacturing costs, excess manufacturing capacity and a downturn in demand for construction machinery due to the economic recession of the early 1980s as reasons for these closures. Labor-related costs in Buchanan amounted to $25.68 per hour for each employee, whereas the hourly costs at Clark's factories in Rockingham and Statesville, North Carolina, were only $14.91. United Auto Workers Union Local 468 offered major wage and benefit cuts, to no avail. The company posted losses of $163.8 million during the first three-quarters of 1982. Closure of the Buchanan and Benton Harbor plants put over 700 employees out of work.

Clark's still maintained its corporate headquarters and some manufacturing in Buchanan, but during the late 1980s and early 1990s that, too, left town. Clark Credit Corporation, the company's financing subsidiary, stayed in Buchanan for several years but eventually pulled out as well. In 1995, Clark (by then only a memory in Buchanan) merged with Ingersoll-Rand and ceased to exist as a distinct corporate identity. Many factors had contributed to Clark's downfall: high labor costs, strikes and bickering with unions; foreign competition; economic recessions; and top management figures who failed to understand Clark, its products and its people.

Whatever the many causes, Clark's departure devastated Buchanan. Entire families had worked for the company; in some cases, Clark had employed several generations of families. Many former employees had no training for anything other than factory work and had to leave town or accept lower-paying jobs. When blue-collar and white-collar jobs at Clark disappeared, so too did the paychecks. The multiplier effect associated with this loss of income spread through the community. Businesses that had depended on the purchasing power of Clark employees closed their doors.

Despite Clark's departure, Buchananites have fond memories of working for the company. Retirees meet to reminisce about their days of working on the factory floor and in the offices. They remember the grand days of working for Clark, their many friends in the Clark family, and the work they did together to build one of America's greatest corporations. Buchanan and the Clark Equipment Company will always be synonymous with each other.

Some of the original George R. Rich Company employees at the Buchanan plant, 1905. Left to right: John Sadler, J. M. Chubb, unknown, unknown, Bert Conant, Charles Storbeck, Joe Havernac, Bob Davis, Art Holmberg, unknown (sitting behind Holmberg), Ed Hill (in light coveralls), unknown (sitting behind Hill), Oscar Anderson (seated at far right). Standing at doorway: Alec Downs, Ira Rich, Oscar Frederickson, Clint Hathaway. *(BCHA Collections)*

Footbridge over McCoy's Creek to the Celfor Tool Company, ca. 1910. *(BCHA Collections)*

The entire office staff of Celfor's drill department posed on the footbridge over McCoy's Creek, 1911. Left to right: Helen Weymouth, Fannie D. Williams, Alta Theresa McDonald, Winifred Morley, Blendina Waterman. *(BCHA Collections)*

Top and bottom: Paving the street at the Celfor Tool Company, ca. 1910. *(BCHA Collections)*

The man who started it all: Eugene B. Clark. He served as president of the company that bore his name from 1916 until his death on July 29, 1942. *(BCHA Collections)*

Work nearing completion on the Celfor Tool Company factory. *(BCHA Collections)*

Workers at the Celfor Tool Company, ca. 1912. *(BHCA Collections)*

Celfor Tool Company, ca. 1910. *(BHCA Collections)*

The Buchanan Electric Steel Company (1910) and the Celfor Tool Company (1906) merged in 1916 to become the Clark Equipment Company. *(BHCA Collections)*

Clark's drill and foundry operations, ca. 1916. *(BCHA Collections)*

Clark's axle shop, ca. 1916. *(BCHA Collections)*

Clark's No. 1 axle shop, ca. 1916. *(BCHA Collections)*

The office staff hard at work in Clark's billing department, ca. 1916. Foundries and factories did not employ women on the shop floor, but women could find work in the company offices. *(BCHA Collections)*

Sandblasting and the annealing oven, ca. 1916. Work in the foundry was hot, filthy and low-paying. *(BCHA Collections)*

Workmen running Bullard boring mills, ca. 1916. *(BCHA Collections)*

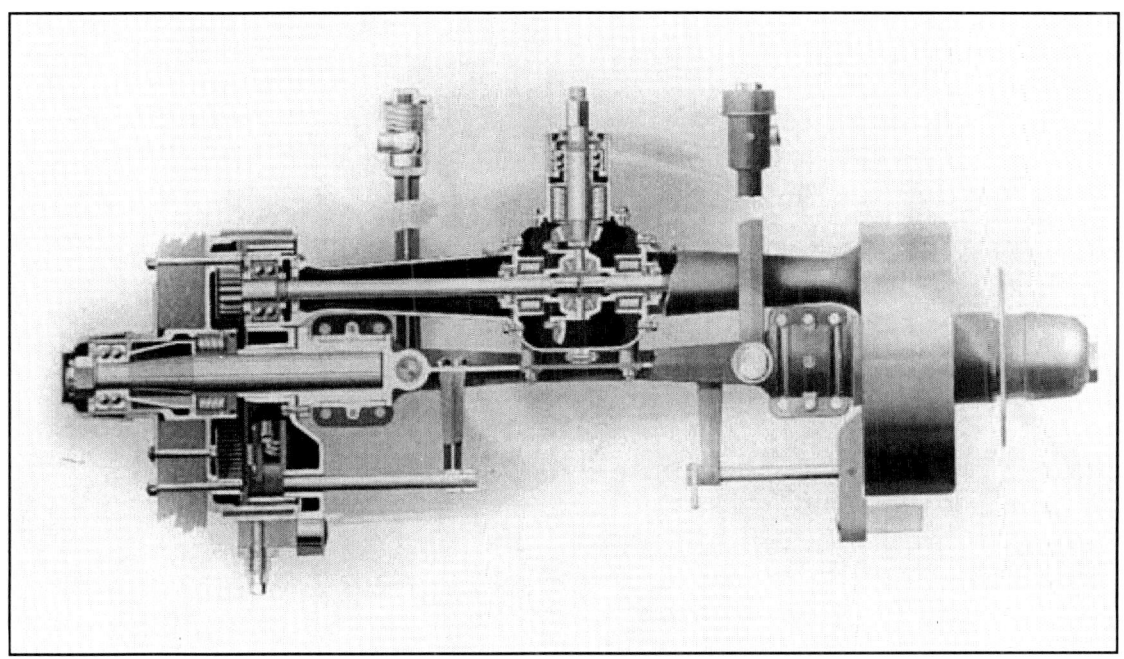

The end result: a Clark Model 2 Axle in a cutaway view showing the myriad parts that went into it. *(BCHA Collections)*

The wheel moulding floor at the Clark foundry, ca. 1916. *(BCHA Collections)*

Axles for World War I army trucks head out of the Clark factory, 1918. *(BCHA Collections)*

"Speed" Ingleright and George Rowe with a pile of axles in Clark's heat treating department, 1920. *(BCHA Collections)*

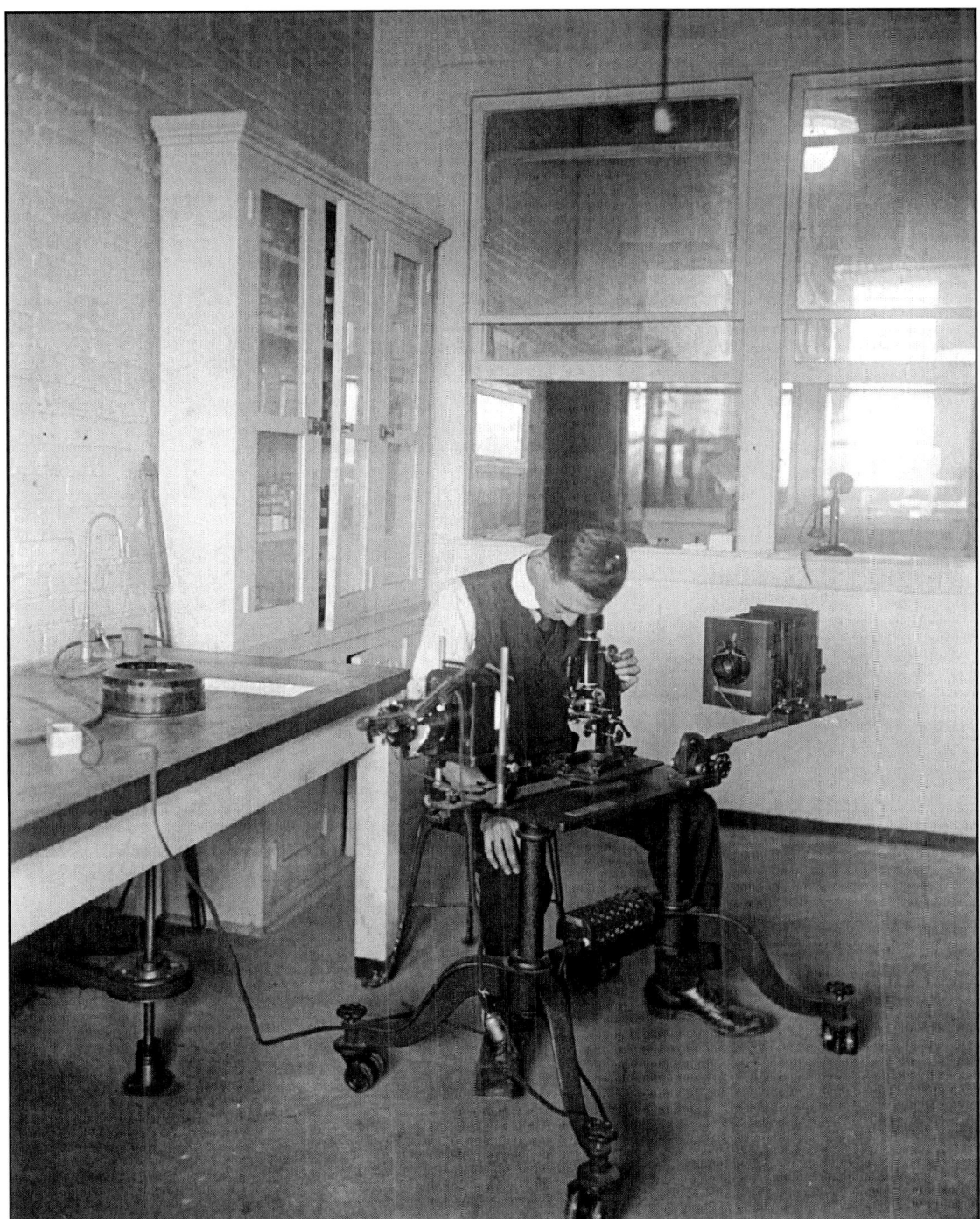

Jack A. White in Clark's chemical laboratory. White joined Clark on New Years' Day 19_4 at age 41. He spent thirty-three years with the company and retired from Clark on New Years' Eve 1946. *(BCHA Collections)*

Working in the foundry, ca. 1920. *(BCHA Collections)*

Loading finished transmission housings in the Clark factory, ca. 1920. *(BCHA Collections)*

"Banjo machine" operators made transmission housings at a wage rate of a dollar an hour. Huge fans blew air over the workmen at the sweltering furnace. *(BCHA Collections)*

Clark Equipment Company's wheel shop, 1919. An overhead line shaft ran the individual machines. *(BCHA Collections)*

A bungalow (top) and American Foursquare in Clark's "Liberty Heights" subdivision, ca. 1920.

The Clark Hospital used a modified Italianate-style house. *(BCHA Collections)*

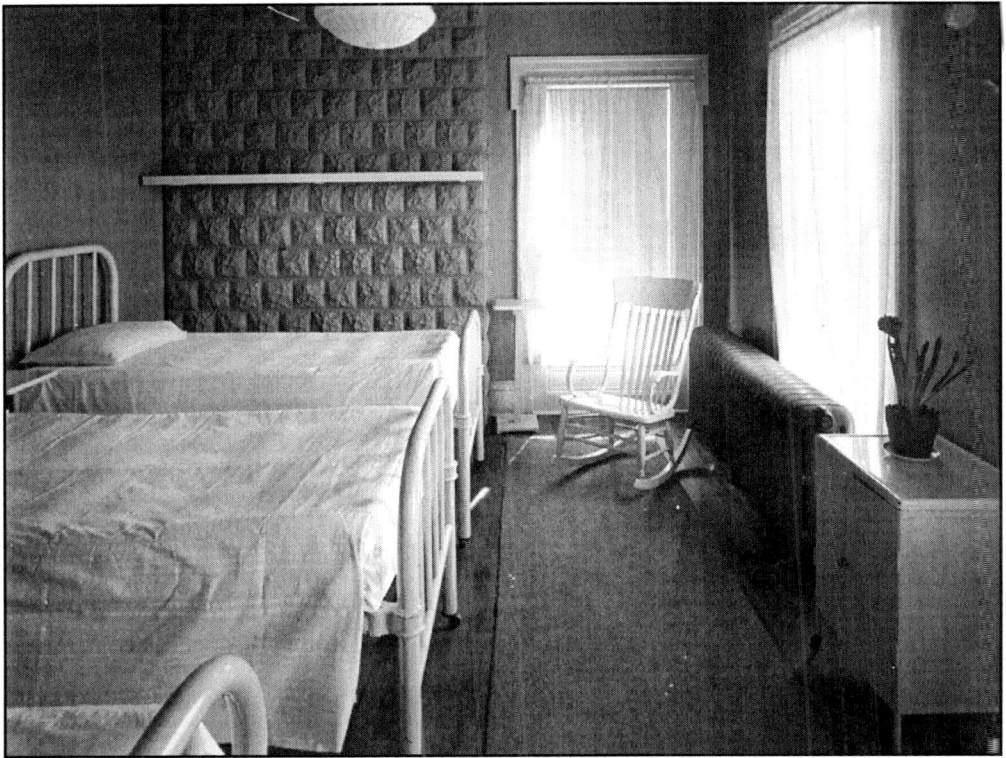

One of the patients' rooms in the Clark Hospital. *(BCHA Collections)*

The Clark Players staged performances in the Clark Theater in shows that entertained people in Buchanan and provided a creative outlet for the cast and crew. A scene from *It Pays to Advertise,* ca. 1920. *(BCHA Collections)*

The Clark Players ham it up in *Nothing But The Truth,* ca. 1920. *(BCHA Collections)*

Clark Equipment Company basketball team, 1920. Team members are Herb Lowe, Ray Stevens, John Volkers, E. Bachman, J. Brown, Charles Brown, Edgar Huebner, Kenneth Murphy, George Murphy and Art Wray. *(BCHA Collections)*

The Clark Equipment Company band togged out in comedic outfits, 1922. *(BCHA Collections)*

Clark Equipment hoped its motorized railroad car, the Autotram, would pull it out of the Great Depression. At its debut in December 1932, Clark President Eugene B. Clark, (right) poses with chief engineer R. J. Burrows. *(BCHA Collections)*

Four national newsreel distributors filmed the Autotram when it rolled out of its birthplace at Clark's Battle Creek plant on December 5, 1932 . The aluminum motorized rail coach was streamlined and air conditioned and designed to hit 85 m.p.h. on standard railbeds. *(BCHA Collections)*

The Autotram takes shape in Clark's Battle Creek factory, 1932. *(BCHA Collections)*

Excited schoolchildren ride on the Autotram, 1932. *(BCHA Collections)*

Grand Trunk Railroad office girls board the Autotram at Battle Creek. Engineer Walter Yeakel leans down from the cab. *(BCHA Collections)*

The Autotram speeds up on the Michigan Central Railroad's main line near Battle Creek, December 1932. *(BCHA Collections)*

The Clark Autotram's passenger cabin as a club lounge, featuring aluminum furniture and special cylindrical aluminum lighting equipment. *(BCHA Collections)*

The Autotram flopped, but the wheel assemblies (trucks) Clark developed for it sold well to street railways. Here a car destined for Coney Island rolls out of Clark's factory in Battle Creek. City streetcars in many North American cities used Clark trucks, including those in Chicago, Pittsburgh, Washington, D. C., San Diego, Vancouver, Brooklyn, Baltimore, Los Angeles and other cities. *(BCHA Collections)*

Above and facing page: A meeting of Celfor employees in the Clark Theater, ca. 1940.

Left section, front row: Leroy Burke, Marvin Hartman, Everett Watson, Art Johnston, Otis Flenar, Fred Zimmerman, Clarence Keene. Second row: Charles Dewey, Gordon Covert, Nels Nordin, William Carlson, Bill Baker, John J. Buckle. Third row: Lee O. Davis, Clair McKee, Bill Jasper, Frank Merson, Ray Babcock, Lloyd Bratton, Eugene Shepherd, Ed Pazder. Fourth row: Eugene Wells, Anton Novak, Al Truhn, Harold ("Boots") Kramer, Al Menzel, Louis Schmidt, Philbert Bilotti, Henry Seem, Ray Gregory. Fifth row: Ellsworth Clem, Roy Fletcher, Phil Birong, Roscoe Raven, Bob Furner, Ted Tees, Lee Allis, Phil Mallen. Sixth row: John Kaufmann, William Thurston, Sam Denno, Jr., Art Pudell, Bob Rose, Al Kettlehut, Frank Rumsey, William Shaw, Russ Wales, William Manspeaker, Dan Taylor. Seventh row: Leo Finney, Harold Heeter, Marion Drietzler, H. A. Slitter, Emory Rader, Joe Wiest, Guy Bruce, John E. Cook, Mitchell Booth, Henry Keller. Eighth row: Sam Denno, Sr., Joe Warner, Lonnie Harrell, Gilbert Renbarger, Ralph Britton, Ernie Grime, Goldie Smith, Harvey Swem, Burell Dunham, Dick Oberholzer. Ninth row: LaVerne Myers, Bennie Bilotti, Clarence Ravish, Don Heiney, Art Zick, Chuck Krieger, Mac Denges, R. J. Wood, Harold Heckathorn, Jake Freehling, John Gowland. Tenth row: Richmond Watson, Al Klute, Chuck Kennedy, Raymond O. Mell, Willis Merrill, Jack Hess, Claude Lauver, Bob Franklin, Chester Collings, Harry Comers.

Right section, front row: Elmer Zilke, Steve Rudoni, Rolland Brado, Cecil Murder, Alvin Utrup, Rolland McMillen, Rollo Chappell. Second row: Lincoln Carlock, Paul Wirtig, Carl Harbaugh, Art Plannger, Ray Guhl, Howard Lougheed, John Nichols, Erv Heirmann, Jr. Third row: Frank Trapp, Garry Clements, Pete Liska, Claude Hess, Burton Benson, Mark Heiney, Fred Hall, Ellsworth Bristol, Bert Daley. Fourth row: William Zackman, George Busie, Ernie Renbarger, Emmett Heiney, Buck Kingery, Tony Hiembuch, Bill Forthman, Edd Howard, Lewis Walls. Fifth row: Edwin Armstrong, Ralph Huston, Jack Wessells, Jim Crill, Moon Somora, Gus Jeschke, M. Watkins, George Smith, Lynn Smith, Al Bowerman. Sixth row: Fred Hewitt, Norman Lee, Herbert Marsh, Lee Conrad, Merle Bromley, Dick Morriss, Bill Gowell, Keith Everman, Harold Renbarger, Russell Allen, Ted Siekman. Seventh row: Lawrence Busse, Wilbur Utrup, Walter Backman, Lyle Mitchell, Jerry Mann, W. T. Beardsley, Dick Backman, Jack Meyers, Stanton Thorpe, Bob Neal. Eighth row: Clarence Canfield, Herman Nitz, Aubrey Sheets, Joe Horak, Godfrey Tucek, Rollie Bunch, Gale Wade, Jack Berg, Don DeFries. Ninth row: Don Clifford, August Nehring, Harry Stewart, Marv Sexton, Dean Franz, Lyle Dunham, John Deere, Lehman Craft, Everett Martin, Donald Andrews. Tenth row: John Kramer, Harold Harper, Emil Rienke, Sr., Harry Smith, Fred Thorson, Harold Ried, Howard Ehlert, Joe Benak. *(BCHA Collections)*

Albert S. Bonner succeeded Eugene B. Clark as company president after Clark died in 1942. He served until his own untimely death from a heart attack in February 1945. *(BCHA Collections)*

The company newsletter, *At Clark's,* celebrated the presentation of the Army-Navy "E" Award to the company on January 31, 1945. The military made the award "for great achievement in the production of war equipment" during World War II. *At Clark's* declared that the "E" banner flying above the Buchanan factory, "belongs to the operators of the lathes, the presses, the cutters, the shapers, to those who feed and tend the furnaces and ovens, to those who man the forges, to the inspector at his bench, the trucker in the aisles, to the stenographer at her typewriter, to the nurse rendering first aid to the injured, to the safety worker who thinks and works to anticipate and prevent the injury, to the executive who co-ordinates operations, to the mail girl who shoulders her pack, to the watchman who carries his clock."

Many Clark products went to war during World War II. Here a "halftrack" runs on Clark axles. The halftrack's African-American crew is unusual, since racism kept most African-Americans out of combat and employed in menial labor. *(BCHA Collections)*

The "Clark-Air" bulldozer, small enough and light enough to fit aboard a C-47 transport plane. "Opel" goes onto a C-47 at an airfield in North Africa on January 13, 1943. Clark built the first Clark-Airs but found that its overtaxed factories could not fill the military's orders for the little bulldozer. It soon licensed another firm to build them. *(BCHA Collections)*

The World War II Allies rode to victory on Clark axles. Here, soldiers assemble the axles to a GMC 2 ½ ton truck – the famed "deuce and-a-half" – somewhere in Australia on December 1, 1942. *(BCHA Collections)*

Clark Equipment established a huge trailer camp as temporary housing for the hundreds of workers who poured into Buchanan during World War II. *(BCHA Collections)*

Clark Chief Executive Officer George Spatta was born and raised in New York City's tough Hell's Kitchen neighborhood. After earning an engineering degree at Cooper Union he got a job with General Electric in 1914. He came to Clark in 1927 and served as the company's CEO from 1945 to 1968. During those years he oversaw Clark's rise to an international manufacturer, with sales climbing from $55 million to nearly $530 million. Spatta died in 1971. *(BCHA Collections)*

The Clark Equipment engineering department in Buchanan, March 1949. First row, front to back: Pat Nagel, Burt Mills, Ronny Bolster, John Borland, Jacob Walls, William Lewis, Wes Strong. Second row: H. W. Hosbein, F. Metz, Don Kilgore, Nelson Ream, Elmer Maynard, M. Hoag. Third row: Mel Drietzler, George Nespital, F. Clem, R. Hawks. *(BCHA Collections)*

An aerial view of Clark's Buchanan factory. *(BCHA Collections)*

Clark tried the market for motor homes during the 1960s with the "Cortez," seen here in an idyllic company publicity photo. *(BCHA Collections)*

Walter E. Schirmer, here in 1963, came to Clark as patent counsel in 1937. He was elected president in 1963 and became president and chairman of the board in 1968. He served as president until 1968 and retired as chairman of the board in 1979. *(BCHA Collections)*

Many Clark employees spent their entire career with the company. Clark honored these men for thirty years' of service: Earle S. Zinninger, Samuel J. McClellan, Charles F. Simpson, Charles F. Bachman and Frank W. Dodge. *(BCHA Collections)*

Clark Equipment bought Ross Carrier of Benton Harbor, which produced a straddle carrier. The Model 100-S, being shown to Clark's board of directors in Buchanan in 1953, had a 45,000 lb. capacity. *(BCHA Collections)*

Forklifts, like this Yardlift 100 being shown in Buchanan in 1953, became a staple Clark product. *(BCHA Collections)*

Clark's "Michigan" line of cranes, like these displayed in Buchanan on
August 7, 1953, worked on construction projects all over the world.
(BCHA Collections)

Lunchtime on the factory floor, 1957. *(BCHA Collections)*

Bert E. Phillips (standing) succeeded Walter Schirmer as president of Clark in 1970 and as chairman of the board in 1979. He retired as board chairman in 1982. *(BCHA Collections)*

A Wagner Loader of the Minerva Oil Company using a Clark Equipment transmission, 1968. *(BCHA Collections)*

Chapter 9
School History

Buchanan's early settlers placed a high value on education and established schools in the township and village at the first opportunity. School District No. 1, in fact was organized in 1838, prior to the village's founding, and originally comprised an area four miles long and two miles wide.

The township's first school, a log building, stood on the west side of McCoy's Creek. Located in the future site of the village, it was probably built in 1838 or 1839. It burned down in 1841, but residents promptly built another schoolhouse in its place. Years later, Jane Mansfield Wagner recalled that the log schoolhouse had formerly served as a blacksmith shop, and that the anvil and bellows still resided in one corner. The building had a door and two windows, and a puncheon floor made of logs split lengthwise and laid smooth side up. Students sat on puncheon benches made of split logs with four legs each. Angelina Bird served as schoolmistress in the log school. Miss Bird, Wagner remembered, was a tall, rather plain-looking woman who tapped a ruler against the door to call class into session.

Americans in the early nineteenth century viewed log buildings as a hallmark of poverty and backwardness, so when John Hamilton platted Buchanan in 1842 residents naturally wanted a wood frame schoolhouse for their children. The village erected a twenty by forty-foot frame schoolhouse on North Main Street in 1843 at a cost of $170. Eggleston Smith presided as the building's first schoolmaster.

Buchanan enjoyed rapid growth during the next decade. The number of school-age children rose from 50 in 1843 to 160 in 1854. Buchanan's school system reorganized and adopted the new concept of a "Union School," which united several small school districts into one larger unit. This allowed the school to hire more teachers and separate the students by grade for more age-appropriate instruction. Ultimately, this created the publicly-funded high schools that allowed students seeking a higher level of education in a public school instead of a private academy. Sometimes termed "the people's high school," the union school system put education within the grasp of all children. A new two-story brick union school, thirty by forty feet in size, went up in 1856 at the then-enormous sum of $4,800. The schoolhouse stood on the northeast corner of West and Second streets. After Admiral George Dewey's 1898 victory over the Spanish fleet during the Spanish-American War, West Street was renamed Dewey Avenue and the school became the Dewey Avenue School.

Buchanan's population soon outgrew its brick school. Buchanan's solution to the overcrowding problem gave the town one of Berrien County's best school buildings. In March 1871, the Buchanan School Board let a $20,000 construction contract for a new brick schoolhouse to local businessman Lorenzo P. Alexander. The school grounds encompassed an entire seven-acre square on the south side of Chicago Street, purchased from Nathaniel B. Collins for $3,500. Architect Perley Hale, Jr., designed the building, and the masonry firm of Charles Snyder & Son began work on a stone foundation in late April or early May. Work continued through the summer and fall of 1871. Alexander missed the agreed-upon completion deadline of December 1, but finished the building by the end of the month. On January 12, 1872, the Buchanan Cornet Band led a procession of students from the old school to the new structure. The sprawling brick school standing alone in its yard reminded Buchananites of a military fortress. With memories of the Civil War still fresh in everyone's mind, they dubbed the new schoolhouse "Fort Sumter."

"Fort Sumter" impressed everyone. The three-story building measured 78 by 80 feet and was capped with a slate roof and a belfry that housed a 403-pound bell purchased from the Chicago hardware firm of Hibbard and Spencer. It contained nine rooms in all: eight recitation rooms and a lecture room. The classrooms could accommodate 540 students. A furnace in the basement heated the building, relieving the schoolmaster of the tiresome chore of lighting a fire in the stove on frosty mornings. Buchananites rightly considered it one of southwest Michigan's best schools.

Buchanan graduated its first high school class on June 1, 1877, in a ceremony held in the Advent Christian Church on Oak Street. The class consisted of Lillie B. Howe, Emma Smith, Fannie Woodworth, Nettie Bainton and Minnie Hamilton. Boys rarely graduated from high school during the late nineteenth century because society and families expected boys to enter the workforce no later than age sixteen. Girls, on the other hand, felt no pressure to earn a living and therefore had the opportunity to better their education. Nevertheless, Asa Ham of South Bend, Indiana, became the first boy to graduate from Buchanan High School in 1878. Graduation from high school was no small accomplishment. Candidates not only had to complete the prescribed course of study but also had to write and present a satisfactory graduation essay. Buchanan High School's quality was such that its graduates could enter college without further examinations.

Buchanan built a new high school in 1922 on the same property as the old school at a cost of $200,000. Builders stripped Fort Sumter of its top two floors, and the truncated structure became a heating plant for the new school. Additions enlarged the school, and in 1992 voters approved an $8 million renovation of the building.

During the 1950s and 1960s, Buchanan's growing population necessitated the construction of three elementary schools. The Dewey Avenue School had served as a grade school for many years, but in 1949 it was deemed unsafe. Moccasin School opened in its place about two blocks away. Buchanan dedicated the new Moccasin School on September 9, 1949. Stark School was built in the Liberty Heights subdivision on the southeast side of town in 1959. Designed by architect H. W. Van Dongen of Benton Harbor and built by the Christman Construction Company of South Bend, the new elementary school was named for life-long Buchanan educator Harold C. Stark. Buchanan's third elementary school, Ottawa, was built in 1966-1967 to replace seven elementary school classrooms still located in the high school building. Ottawa featured fourteen rooms, including a multi-purpose room, library and kindergarten. School officials considered naming the new school in honor of famed Buchanan aviator Jack Knight, but finally decided on "Ottawa" so that residents could immediately identify its Ottawa Street location.

Rural residents in the Buchanan area had enjoyed the use of many country schools – typically the so-called "one room schools." A necessity in the days before automobiles, school buses and improved roads allowed students to travel long distances to attend school, these one-room schools dotted the rural landscape around Buchanan. These schools included Miller (No. 2); Broceus (No. 3); Coveney (No. 4); Wagner (No. 5); Colvin (No. 6); Kelsey (No. 7); and Indian Hills (No. 8). Schools in adjacent townships also served many Buchanan-area students, including Kansas (Bertrand No. 2); Howe (Bertrand No. 6); Womer (Bertrand No. 4); and Gardner (Weesaw No. 4). Although limited in curricula and presided over by teachers who often had little formal training, the country schools usually provided a high-quality education. Younger students overheard the older children's lessons and absorbed some of the information. Older students helped their younger counterparts, reinforcing the information that they had learned in previous years. Children from the same families – and often extended families – went to school in the same room, which helped build a strong sense of community in the rural areas.

The one-room schools closed down in the mid-twentieth century. Large central schools, like Buchanan High School, offered advanced curricula that the small country schools could not match. Students entering a more demanding workplace or heading off to college needed a higher level and variety of classes than the one-room school could provide. Families abandoned the little schools when school buses allowed them to send their children to the town schools. The Howe School in Bertrand Township, for example, closed in 1966 when its enrollment dropped below the thirty-five students that the school needed to continue receiving full state support.

The Gardner School in Bertrand Township survives to the present time and remains in use by the Buchanan school system. Built about 1870 at the corner of Gardner and Wagner roads, it closed in 1942 when its few remaining students transferred to the Galien School. Frank Schreier donated the building to the Buchanan School Farm in 1931. The School Farm had the building moved to its property on Andrews Road and restored it as a living history site. Students attend the school once again, but not on a daily basis. Instead, they visit the school for special field trips when their teachers take them there to experience life in a one-room school.

At this writing, Buchanan enjoys an outstanding public educational system. Younger students attend Moccasin, Stark or Ottawa Elementary Schools. They advance to the Buchanan Middle School, constructed in 1974 at a cost of $1.8 million, and then attend Buchanan High School. Enrollment declined slightly during the 1990s, but increased in 2004 due in part to students transferring to Buchanan after Galien High School graduated its final class in the spring of 2004. Buchanan's school system continues the tradition of outstanding education that its early settlers started in the 1830s.

The Dewey Avenue School ca. 1890. Built in 1856, the school became known as the Dewey Avenue School after West Street's name was changed to honor Admiral George Dewey. *(Courtesy Buchanan District Library)*

Students pose in front of the Dewey Avenue School in an undated photograph. *(Courtesy Buchanan District Library)*

May Haller, first grade teacher at the Dewey Avenue school in the 1880s. *(Courtesy Buchanan District Library)*

The Dewey Avenue School in 1945. *(Dale E. Florey Collection)*

Buchanan's first high school, built in 1871-1872. Local residents dubbed the brick structure "Fort Sumter," deeming its massive scale reminiscent of the famed Civil War fort. Architect Perley Hale, Jr., gave the building a mansard roof – the distinctive architectural feature of the Second Empire-style. *(Courtesy Buchanan District Library)*

Buchanan High School's first graduates, the Class of 1877. Lillie B. Howe, Minnie Hamilton, Emma Smith, Fannie Woodworth and Nettie Bainton (posed left to right with teachers Miss Leach and Professor Ray) received their diplomas on June 1, 1877. Graduating from high school at that time required the candidates to take special examinations and to write (and present publicly) an acceptable thesis. *(Courtesy Buchanan District Library)*

Students at Buchanan High School in 1880.

Students at Buchanan High School, ca. 1880. *(Courtesy Buchanan District Library)*

The Buchanan High School Class of 1887 pose with their diplomas on July 18, 1888. Seated left to right: Lura Pears, Mary Hinman, Mabel Smith and Georgia Tichenor; standing: Minnie Spencer, Mary Reynolds, Fred Tichenor, Lottie DeMott and Anna Simmons. *(Courtesy Buchanan District Library)*

The Buchanan 8th grade class in 1889-1890. Back row: Frank Mutchler, Harry Perrott, Milton Platts, Florence Hartsell (teacher), Ivan Hoag, Rossie Harner, Gene Boyle, Frank Redden. Second row from back: Claude Roe, Rob Franklin, Lottie Rundell, Cora Dumbolton, Dot Barnes, Hattie Sweeney, Ed Frye, Bert Bailey, Earl Light, Guy Williams, Lloyd Dumbolton, Charles Boyle. Third row from back: Allie Spencer, Anna Wilbur, "Biddie" Blodgett, Billie Strauser, Lillie Pears, Edith Spinnetta, Emma Eisele, Daisy Croupe, Mary Koontz, Adah Rough, Eliza Arney, Lillie Mutchler. Front row: Mabel Redden, Viola Conrad, Mabel Hoag, Carrie Hamilton, Jennie Beistle, Allie Kinney, Jennie Bailey, Daisy Richards, Anna Weaver, Maude Welch, Adah Kingery, Susie Butler, Ada Slocum.

Only six of these students - Jennie Beistle, Lloyd Dumbolton, Ed Frye, Earl Light, Ada Slocum and Claude Roe - would go on to graduate from high school in 1894. *(Courtesy Buchanan District Library)*

"Fort Sumter" on a cold winter day. *(Courtesy Donald F. Ryman Collection)*

The Buchanan High School Class of 1893. Graduates are, left to right: May Zerbe, Henry C. Eisele, Lillie Andrews, Nellie E. Miller, Ed Swain, Bernice E. Earl, Nettie Drake, Charles A. Montague and Mattie Straw. *(Courtesy Buchanan District Library)*

The Buchanan High School Class of 1894. Back row, left to right: Lloyd Dumbleton, Claude Roe, Harry Brunson, Earl Light and Ed Fry. Middle row: Ada Slocum, Daisy L. V. Emery, Mae Wilson, Addie Kelsey and Jennie Beistle. Front row: Lottie Thayer, Elmer Beistle and May Brewer. *(Courtesy Buchanan District Library)*

High school students on the steps of "Fort Sumter" with Supt. Mr. Moore at far right. *(Courtesy Buchanan District Library)*

Buchanan High School graduating class of 1896. Graduates with their diplomas piled in front are Lucile B. Weese, J. Clyde DeViney, Bessie L. Light, Ethel L. Woodbridge, Edgar L. Kelsey, Winifred M. Noble, Frank H. Thayer, Anna Wilbur, George A. Conrad, Elizabeth Southerton, William C. L. Rough, Louise A. Northam, Martha E. Scott, Nina D. Holliday and Luenette F. Batchelor. *(Courtesy Buchanan District Library)*

The seventh grade class at the Buchanan High School in 1898. The teacher, Ann Treat, stands at far right. *(Courtesy Buchanan District Library)*

The Buchanan High School graduating class of 1896. Graduates, with their diplomas piled in front, are Lucile B. Weese, J. Clyde DeViney, Bessie L. Light, Ethel L. Woodbridge, Edgar L. Kelsey, Winifred M. Noble, Frank H. Thayer, Anna Wilbur, George A. Conrad, Elizabeth Southerton, William C. L. Rough, Louise A. Northam, Martha E. Scott, Nina D. Holliday and Luenette F. Batchelor. *(Courtesy Buchanan District Library)*

Buchanan students on the high school steps. Gladys Webb stands second from the right in the front row; other students are unidentified. *(Courtesy Buchanan District Library)*

A Buchanan first grade class, 1898. *(Courtesy Buchanan District Library)*

The Buchanan High School Class of 1898. Students are Jennie Churchill, Minnie Sawyer, Eli Conrad (who died in November 1898), Frank C. Merson, Jay M. Glover, Harry Zerbe, Carson French, Robert Richards, Paul Plimpton, Maxson Chubb, Charles Dumbolton, Robert Henderson, Earl Kramer and Arthur Wray. Not pictured: William Rose. *(Courtesy Buchanan District Library)*

A Buchanan sixth grade class in 1907. *(Courtesy Buchanan District Library)*

A group of unidentified students at Buchanan High School, 1909. *(Courtesy Buchanan District Library)*

Students on the steps of the Buchanan High School, ca. 1908. Front row: Nettie Stopp; unknown; unknown; Harold Roe; Virgil Swartz; unknown; unknown; unknown; unknown; unknown; unknown. Second row: Blanche Williams Heim; Winifred Bradley; unknown; Florence Keller; Earl Waterman; unknown; unknown; unknown; unknown; unknown; unknown; Mildred Roe; Agnes McFallon; Irene Fuller; Reba Binns Lamb; _____ Lentz; unknown; Ruth Reese Marsh; unknown. Third row: Rose Hershman; Mae Smith; Bernice Ferguson; James Phillips. Fourth row: Louise Arney; Ruby Eldridge; Iva McGowan. Fifth row: Bessie Davis; Hallie Boone; Minta Wagner; Irene Troutfetter; Myrtle Blodgett; Hildred Camp; Winifred Morley; unknown; unknown; unknown; unknown; unknown; unknown. Back row: Georgia Barnhart; unknown; Cora Hess Boone; unknown; Grace Fowler; Ward Hamilton; unknown; _____ Stopp; unknown; unknown; Minnie Blodgett; Frances Taber. *(Courtesy Buchanan District Library)*

Buchanan High School, "Fort Sumter," in 1918. *(Courtesy Buchanan District Library)*

The new Buchanan High School, ca. 1925. *(Courtesy Buchanan District Library)*

Unidentified group of Buchanan students. *(Courtesy Buchanan District Library)*

The Buchanan High School Class of 1904, apparently at a class reunion, ca. 1940. *(Courtesy Buchanan District Library)*

Chapter 10 – Churches

Buchanan has a history of religious organizations that dates back to the founding of the village. Churches played an important part in community life. They provided not only religious instruction and inspiration but also served as social centers. Village residents made friends among members of their church congregations and looked forward to a day of rest after a long workweek. Churches in the village bound the community together, but also allowed the residents to enjoy a degree of diversity in their religious worship. Buchanan's churches represent nearly every major Christian denomination.

Methodist Episcopal Church

Methodists founded the first church in Buchanan. In 1831, the family of John and Martha Hunter moved to Niles Township and joined a Methodist Church that had started there. The Hunters hosted prayer meetings in their home, out of which formed a church class. In 1842, this Methodist class formed the nucleus of a group that met in Buchanan at the home of the class leader, David Sanford. For many years the Methodist congregation met in private homes and the Buchanan schoolhouses.

In 1853, the Methodists took a five-year lease on the Presbyterian Church for its services. In 1860, the congregation constructed the village's first Methodist Church on the southwest corner of Days Avenue and Smith Street. The house next door served as the parsonage, or manse. The Methodists took justifiable pride in having Buchanan's first brick church. As time passed, however, the church membership grew until by 1880 it numbered 100 people and the Sunday School membership topped 150.

In 1907, the congregation decided to replace the church with a new, larger building in a more convenient location. A building committee consisting of Albert A. Worthington, E. J. Stopp and Dr. James A. Garland let a construction contract for $8,000 to Wilson Leiter, who razed the old church building for its lumber. Isaac M. Vincent donated land at the corner of Oak and Roe streets on which to build the new church. Construction began in January 1907 and ended with the dedication of the new church in late August. The Richardsonian Romanesque structure included a grand pipe organ, oak pews and cork flooring. That new marvel, electric lights, lit up the interior so that, as the *Berrien County Record* newspaper enthused, "it appears as if balls of living fire were suspended from the ceilings. . . ." Magnificent stained-glass windows, the gift of local businessman William A. Palmer, ornamented the sanctuary. This building still stands as the Methodist Episcopal Church.

Faith United Methodist Church

Although not the first congregation established in Buchanan, the Church of the United Brethren holds the distinction of having built the city's first church. Rev. Josiah Terrel and Rev. Babcock organized the church around 1846 with six charter members. The congregation held services in the home of John Hatfield and in a carding mill until 1849, when it built a church. A series of circuit-riding pastors preached at the church until 1866, when it became a mission church and Rev. George Sickafoose came to stay.

The United Brethren Church merged with the Evangelical Church in 1946. The latter congregation originated in 1888, when several residents of Portage Prairie moved to Buchanan and decided to start a church. The thirteen original members organized the Buchanan Society of the Evangelical Association (later renamed the First Evangelical Church) on March 14, 1888, at the home of William R. and Mary Ann Rough. Rev. Jacob A. Frye, pastor of the Portage Prairie Church, had charge of the organization. The congregation held its first business meetings in the Rough Brothers Wagon Works office. Regular preaching services were held in Rough Brothers Hall (the opera house) while the congregation built a new brick church building on the southeast corner of North Oak Street and First (now Dewey) Street. The church was dedicated on November 11, 1888. Rev. Frye became the church's second pastor, serving from 1889 to 1890.

The church celebrated its fiftieth anniversary in 1938 and completed extensive improvements and remodeling of the building. A new Wicks pipe organ, donated to replace the old pump organ, was dedicated on August 3, 1947.

On August 27, 1961, the church broke ground for a new building at 728 North Detroit Street. The congregation held its first services in the new church building on November 4, 1962, and observed dedication services on October 6, 1963. Denominational mergers led the church to change its name to the First Evangelical United Brethren Church in 1946; in 1968, it became the Faith United Methodist Church. The Buchanan Lodge of the Free and Accepted Masons bought the original 1888 church building and continues to use it at this writing.

Advent Christian Church

The Advent Christian Church numbered among Buchanan's most prominent religious institutions in the late nineteenth century. The denomination originated with William Miller of Vermont, whose study of the Old Testament prophesies convinced him that Jesus Christ would return to Earth in 1843 or 1844. Millerism caught on throughout much of New England and New York, and by the spring of 1844 the movement numbered over one thousand congregations with some fifty thousand members. One of Miller's converts, Samuel Snow, calculated that Christ's return would occur on October 22, 1844. Many Millerites quit their jobs and sold their property in anticipation of the imminent Day of Judgment. Disappointment crushed many of the believers when that day came and went without incident. Many Millerites left the movement, but others pinned their faith on the hope of Christ's return rather than the day itself. Out of this group of believers eventually emerged the Advent Christian Church and the Seventh-day Adventist Church.

The Advent Christians built a church building in about 1855, then constructed a second one in 1866-1867 on the first block of South Oak Street. The church had started around 1851, when Rev. Daniel R. Mansfield and his wife, Mary, moved to Buchanan from Union Mills, Indiana, and borrowed the United Brethren Church to hold Adventist services. A congregation formed and held Saturday services in the United Brethren Church and a hotel ballroom. Rev. J. R. Lister served as the church's first pastor.

The Advent Church soon became Buchanan's largest religious institution, with a membership of 282 people in the early 1860s. Buchanan became the denomination's publishing center in 1871. The Western Advent Publishing Association produced a weekly entitled *The Advent Times,* which enjoyed a circulation of 4,500, and the *Advent Christian Quarterly,* which went out to 1,200 subscribers. Despite its early popularity, the Advent Christian Church disbanded in the early 1920s. The church building later saw use as a business site, the Pattern Works, and was razed in 1957.

First Presbyterian Church

On May 22, 1847, when the town was not quite five years old, a group of residents met at the home of Uriel Enos to explore the idea of founding a Presbyterian Church. The meeting ended with the appointment of Enos, Jacob D. Dutton and Charles Baker to a committee to secure ministerial assistance for that purpose. With the aid of Rev. Luther Humphrey and Rev. P. S. Pratt, the group organized the First Presbyterian Church of

Buchanan on June 19. One dozen people made up the original congregation. Rev. Porter B. Parry, a Congregationalist minister, served as supply pastor from October 1847 until February 1853. The congregation built a church on Third Street in 1849-1850, but membership failed to grow and Buchanan's Methodists leased the building for five years during the 1850s. The Presbyterians, in the meantime, met in members' homes. Membership dwindled to sixteen people. The church languished until 1859, when the Presbytery of Kalamazoo appointed Rev. Elisha B. Sherwood to revitalize its Buchanan church. Under Rev. Sherwood's leadership, the congregation went about recruiting more members. Buchananites began to join the church, Rev. Sherwood became the full-time pastor, and in 1859 the Presbyterians reoccupied their church building. By 1880, the church boasted a membership of 120 people.

Larger attendance every Sunday soon necessitated the construction of a larger church. A new brick building went up in 1892. Like their Methodist neighbors, church members took pride in their building's stained-glass windows and pipe organ. A fire destroyed the church on December 19, 1924, and for the next three years the congregation held Sunday services in the American Legion meeting rooms above the City Hall. The Presbyterians dedicated their new church building in 1927, which was built under the leadership of Rev. Harry Staver. That building, located at 115 West Front Street, still serves as the First Presbyterian Church. The church built a new education wing in the spring of 1966 on the building's south side. The wing provided space for a fellowship hall, nine classrooms and a nursery.

Buchanan Church of Christ

The Buchanan Church of Christ originated on December 17, 1854, when several Buchanan residents met in the village schoolhouse to organize a church of that denomination. The impetus for the church's creation had come from Dr. John M. Roe, who had moved to Buchanan in 1851 to practice medicine. The good doctor persuaded his brother, twenty-four year-old William M., to move from South Bend, Indiana, to his new town and establish a Church of the Disciples of Christ. Seventeen people enrolled as members on that first day in 1854.

The congregation flourished. Church members held services in the town schoolhouse until September 18, 1859, when they dedicated a new church building on West Third Street. Members of the congregation did most of the construction work themselves: Charles Roe hauled lumber for the building from his sawmill north of town, and Everett McCollum and Eli Roe Jr. (John and William's brother) handled the carpentry. William M. Roe served as pastor until 1866. When he left, the Church of Christ boasted a membership of about 250 people. During his tenure with the Buchanan church, Rev. Roe had also found time to publish a book, *Bible vs. Materialism* (1859), and organize another dozen churches in the area.

Several name changes also took place during the church's history. Originally the Disciples of Christ, it became the First Christian Church of Buchanan in 1908 and the Church of Christ in 1968. The church building itself underwent extensive remodeling in 1899 and 1914.

Fire destroyed the original Church of Christ building on February 11, 1940. The congregation immediately set to work to erect a new structure, and let a construction contract to the firm of Bradley Brothers Builders. The congregation dedicated its new brick church on Sunday, November 17, 1940. Later construction projects included an educational wing, built in 1957, and a new sanctuary and fellowship hall, dedicated in November 1969.

Buchanan Seventh-day Adventist Church

The Buchanan Seventh-day Adventist Church was first organized as a part of the West Michigan Conference of Seventh-day Adventists on October 5, 1907, with a charter membership of nineteen people. In 1921, it bought the building formerly occupied by the Larger Hope Church of Christ on the northeast corner of Moccasin and Third streets. This first SDA church disbanded in 1937, and then reorganized as a part of the Michigan Conference of Seventh-day Adventists on December 2, 1939. The reorganized church used the original frame building. Church membership grew in the 1940s and early 1950s with the assistance of students and pastors from Emmanuel Missionary College (now Andrews University) in Berrien Springs. When the Church of Christ offered to purchase the church building in 1954, the Adventist congregation decided to erect a new, larger church on the east edge of town on the Niles-Buchanan Road. Volunteers from the congregation pitched in and built most of the new brick church themselves. They dedicated the new building on August 1, 1959. An addition built in 1976 provided larger facilities for the congregation. Because the Adventists hold their weekly services on Saturdays, they have made their church available to other denominations on Sundays.

In 1962, the Adventists established a center in the upstairs rooms over the Roti-Roti shoe store on Front Street to collect clothes and food for those in need. This community program soon needed a larger facility, so the church bought and remodeled a house at 205 Days Avenue for the purpose. The church operated the facility until declining need allowed it to sell the building in 1972 and transfer the service to the church or other facilities.

St. Anthony's Catholic Church

One Sunday in 1908, Father Koenig looked out at his congregation in Dayton, near Buchanan, and saw only one person: Mary Kann. The dismayed priest decided then and there that he would form a church in the more populous town of Buchanan.

Dayton's Catholic church had been built during the Civil War. Local farmers and Buchanan residents both attended the church. Father John Cappon from the Bertrand Mission trudged eight miles each way along the Michigan Central Railroad tracks every Sunday to celebrate Mass there.

Father Koenig opened the Catholic Church without a building. For two years, the priest held services in the home of Henry R. and Lolieda Adams, and then rented the Grand Army of the Republic hall. About 1910, the Rev. Father John Welch found himself assigned to the Three Oaks Catholic Church and to missions in New Buffalo, Sawyer and Buchanan. Father Welch rented the Larger Hope Church for services, and then bought a lot on the corner of South Detroit Street and Whitman Court on which to build a church. Bishop Gallagher dedicated and laid the cornerstone for St. Anthony's Catholic Church in November 1911.

St. Paul's Lutheran Church

Although Lutheran churches had an early start in other areas of Berrien County, Buchanan had none until the Redeemer Lutheran Mission opened in 1928 as a preaching station. Rev. Otto E. Sohn, then the pastor of St. Paul's Lutheran Church in Niles, led the services. After Rev. Sohn answered a call to serve in Flint, Michigan, the Niles church welcomed Rev. Theodore Laesch as its new pastor. Rev. Laesch, like Rev. Sohn, served the congregation in Buchanan as well. Under his leadership, Buchanan's Lutherans organized St. Paul's Lutheran Church on November 19, 1933, with eighteen charter members.

Until 1945, the church held services in private homes and above a store in a room that had formerly housed the law office of attorney William Desenberg. The church then bought a grand old Italianate mansion on Front Street. Businessman Leander P. Fox, part owner of the Zinc Collar Pad Company, had built the house in 1851. The Lutherans remodeled the house as a church and converted the second floor into living quarters for the pastor. Rev. Fred G. Wilkins became the church's first resident pastor in 1947; he would serve the church for the next thirty-two years.

The old Fox House fell to the wrecking ball in 1950 when it was razed to make way for a new church building and parsonage. The congregation moved into its new quarters in December 1951, and held dedication services on July 20, 1952. St. Paul's marked another milestone in 1958, when the church became self-supporting and no longer needed the subsidy furnished by the Michigan District Mission Board.

Church of the Nazarene

Like many of Buchanan's churches, the Church of the Nazarene held its first services in members' homes. Sunday school classes for the denomination began in the spring of 1944 and grew large enough that the congregation sought out rented quarters in Buchanan's business district. Rev. Pearle Crane came to the church later in 1944, and in March of the following year helped formally organize the church.

The congregation soon built a church on the corner of Moccasin and Fourth streets and moved into its new building in November 1945.

Other Churches

Despite the city's size, Buchanan has no non-Christian religious institutions. It does not, for example, host an Islamic temple or Jewish synagogue. Nevertheless, Buchanan area residents have their choice of attending many churches in the community. These include the Porter Community African Methodist Episcopal Church, the Christian Life Center, the New Good Hope Baptist Church, the Wildwood Baptist Church, the First Missionary Baptist Church, St. Matthews Missionary Baptist Church, the Faith Victory Fellowship Church, Bethel Apostolic Tabernacle, and the Jehovah's Witnesses.

The Bethany Class of the Methodist Sunday school, 1916. *(Courtesy Buchanan District Library)*

The Methodist Episcopal Church on Days Avenue and Smith Street, ca. 1907. Built in 1860, this fine brick church served the congregation until 1907, when it was replaced with a new church on the corner of Oak and Roe streets. *(Courtesy Buchanan District Library)*

A construction crew at work building the roof of the new Methodist Church in the spring of 1907. On the roof are Charles Blodgett (second from left), Wilson Leiter (fourth from left) and Edgar Ham (right, standing on brickwork). *(Courtesy Buchanan District Library)*

Buchanan's Methodist Episcopal Church, constructed at a cost of $8,000 in 1907. Buchanan architectural historian Donald F. Ryman notes that the church structure includes such details as quatrefoil and trefoils in oak at the ends of the roof supporting timbers, interior ionic columns supporting the choir and organ loft and beadboard wainscoting in the sanctuary. *(Courtesy Buchanan District Library)*

[242]

The Methodist Episcopal Church on the corner of Oak and Roe streets, built in 1907 and photographed ca. 1920. *(Courtesy Berrien County Record)*

The United Brethren Church in Buchanan, built in 1849 when the Greek Revival style of architecture was at its height. *(Courtesy Buchanan District Library)*

A group of women admire new pews for the United Brethren Church. *(Courtesy Buchanan District Library)*

Rev. George Sickafoose and his wife, Matilda Ellen. Rev. Sickafoose became the first pastor of Buchanan's Church of the United Brethren in 1866. He lived in Buchanan until his death on 27 November 1900. Matilda lived in Buchanan until she died in 1911. *(Courtesy Buchanan District Library)*

Rev. Jacob A. Frye helped organize the United Brethren Church and in 1889 became its second pastor. *(Courtesy Faith United Methodist Church)*

The sanctuary of the First Evangelical Church, formerly the United Brethren Church, decorated for Children's Day. *(Courtesy Buchanan District Library)*

Buchanan's First Evangelical Church, ca. 1900. The church building was dedicated on November 11, 1888, and stood on the corner of North Oak and First streets. *(Courtesy Berrien County Record)*

The sanctuary of the First Evangelical Church in 1938. *(Courtesy Faith United Methodist Church)*

Rev. Franklin C. Berger and his wife. Rev. Berger served at the Evangelical Church, later the Faith United Methodist Church, from 1895 to 1899. Born September 16, 1861, in Lima, Indiana, Rev. Berger pastored several churches in the Michigan Conference beginning in 1885. In 1920, he transferred to the Indiana conference, where he pastored until his retirement. He died in 1947. *(Courtesy Buchanan District Library)*

Rev. John R. Niergarth, who served at Buchanan's Evangelical Church from 1899-1903 was born September 7, 1868. He served several other Michigan Evangelical churches, beginning when he transferring from the Washington Conference in 1895. He retired from the ministry in 1938. *(Courtesy Buchanan District Library)*

The Evangelical Church ca. 1960 after it had become the Evangelical United Brethren
Church. *(Dale E. Florey Collection)*

Rev. F. C. Watters, pastor of the Evangelical Church from 1905 to 1907. *(Courtesy Buchanan District Library)*

Riverside camp meeting grounds. The Michigan Conference of the United Methodist Church sold Riverside Camp in 1974. The campground became the site of the White Oaks condominiums. *(Courtesy Buchanan District Library)*

Riverside Camp originated in August 1891, when members of the Portage Prairie and Buchanan Evangelical churches held camp meetings under the leadership of Rev. Jacob A. Frye. In 1892, the churches incorporated Riverside Camp Meeting and bought land along the St. Joseph River on the northeast side of Buchanan. Riverside Camp hosted boys' and girls' camps and a variety of summer camp meetings. *(Courtesy Buchanan District Library)*

Riverside Camp, ca. 1920. *(Courtesy Buchanan District Library)*

Services of Dedication

FIRST EVANGELICAL UNITED BRETHREN CHURCH
720 N. Detroit Street
Buchanan, Michigan

October 5-6, 1963

Dedication program for the new First Evangelical United Brethren Church. It would become the Faith United Methodist Church five years later. *(Courtesy Faith United Methodist Church)*

The Advent Christian Church, built in 1866-1867 on S. Oak Street. The building served as the home of the Pattern Works after the church congregation disbanded in the early 1920s. It was razed in 1957. *(Courtesy Buchanan District Library)*

Buchanan's First Presbyterian Church, ca. 1910. This church, built in 1892, was lost to a fire on December 19, 1924. *(Courtesy Buchanan District Library)*

Construction of Buchanan's first Presbyterian Church began in 1892 at 115 West Front Street. The congregation dedicated the new building on March 3, 1893. The church burned down in 1924 and was replaced with a new structure three years later. *(Courtesy Buchanan District Library)*

An early photograph of the Presbyterian Church, probably taken soon after its construction in 1927. *(Courtesy Berrien County Record)*

St. Anthony's Catholic Church on the corner of South Detroit Street and Whitman Court, ca. 1912. *(Courtesy Buchanan District Library)*

St. Anthony's Catholic Church, ca. 1925. *(Courtesy Berrien County Record)*

Methodist Episcopal Church in Dayton, ca. 1920. *(Courtesy Berrien County Record)*

Chapter 11
Leisure: Buchanan At Play

As the photographic record attests, Buchananites enjoy a good time. The area lakes and St. Joseph River afford good fishing opportunities. As in the 19th century, Buchananites and tourists still enjoy boating and canoeing on the river and at Clear Lake.

Fraternal and business organizations abound. During the 19th and early 20th centuries, Buchanan men joined the Independent Order of Odd Fellows, the Elks Club, the Modern Woodmen of America, or one of the town's three Masonic Lodges. Although many of these organizations have disappeared, others have taken their place. The Buchanan Moose Lodge No. 449, the Buchanan Lions Club, the Niles-Buchanan Service League and the Niles-Buchanan Rotary Club offer opportunities for socializing and helping with civic improvements. Many area veterans have joined the American Legion's Ralph Rumbaugh Post No. 51. The Buchanan Lodge, No. 68, of the Free and Accepted Masons undoubtedly ranks as the oldest of Buchanan's fraternal orders, dating back to its founding on January 13, 1854.

During the early 20th century, the Clark Equipment Company sponsored many recreational activities for its employees and the general public. Musicians played in the Clark Band and athletes played on Clark sports teams. Amateur thespians acted onstage with the Clark Players at the Clark Theater. Although Clark Equipment's clubs and activities have vanished from the town social scene, other groups have taken their place. Among others, the Tin Shop Theater presents community theatrical productions in, appropriately enough, the town's old tin shop. The Tin Shop Theater originated in 1992 as a joint project of the Buchanan Area Foundation (now the Michigan Gateway Community Foundation) and the Buchanan Fine Arts Council. The Tin Shop presents live dramatic productions each summer.

High school sports enjoy enormous popularity in Buchanan. Fans flock to the high school for football, basketball and baseball games. Thousands of students have played on Buchanan school sports teams over the years, and the "Buchanan Bucks" have amassed an enviable record. The boys' basketball team is tied with ten other Michigan teams for the most wins in a single season: 28 in 1975-1976. The boys' team also earned the state record for the highest-scoring Class C semi-final game when they scored 96 points against Iron Mountain in 1978. In girls' basketball, Letitia Bowen ranks 7th in Michigan in points scored during a single season: 759 in 1990. In track and field events, Ryan Harris holds the Michigan Class C record for the 100-meter dash: 10.72 seconds in 1996.

Wilson's Bowling Team, March 12, 1941. Bowling had an unsavory reputation in the 19th century, and many Berrien County towns banned it altogether. It had become well enough accepted by the 20th century, however, that even women could participate. *(Courtesy Buchanan District Library)*

McCoy's Creek beckoned invitingly to boys who wanted to cool off on hot summer days. *(Courtesy Buchanan District Library)*

Fishing was a popular leisure activity in Buchanan, with the St. Joseph River and many lakes near at hand. Jack Miller shows off an impressive catch of fish at Clear Lake, 1895. *(Courtesy Buchanan District Library)*

Unidentified group at Fish Lake, ca. 1915. *(Courtesy Buchanan District Library)*

Clear Lake, west of Buchanan, offered endless summer amusement. *(Courtesy Buchanan District Library)*

Tennis players at Clear Lake's Coney Beach Hotel, 1898. *(Courtesy Buchanan District Library)*

Tightrope walking at Clear Lake, 1895. The Coney Beach Hotel is in the background. *(Courtesy Buchanan District Library)*

"Fun on St. Joseph River," ca. 1910. In the photograph are Cora Rough, Mae and Ellis Roe and Dr. Filman. *(Courtesy Buchanan District Library)*

A group of bathers cool off at Clear Lake, July 12, 1896. *(Courtesy Buchanan District Library)*

Fuller's Pavilion at Clear Lake, ca. 1910. *(Courtesy Berrien County Record)*

Swimming in the area lakes was not just a summer activity. "Polar Bear" Albert Green takes a dip, ca. 1950. *(Courtesy Berrien County Record)*

Milt Curtis and Phil Carlin show off a catch of Northern Pike, September 1969. *(Courtesy Berrien County Record)*

Members of Buchanan's Independent Order of Odd Fellows Lodge in full regalia, 1895. The I.O.O.F. was founded in 17th century England where men who had organized for the unusual purpose of benefiting their fellow human beings were called "odd fellows." America's first I.O.O.F. lodge organized in Baltimore, Maryland, in 1819. It became the first fraternal order to admit women when it adopted the Rebekah Degree in 1851, a document written by South Bend native and future U. S. vice president, Schuyler Colfax. The Buchanan Odd Fellows, Lodge 75, organized on August 2, 1855. The first Rebekah lodge in Buchanan, Lodge 46, was founded in 1871 but closed in 1878. Bay Leaf Rebekah Lodge opened in 1895.

Members of the Independent Order of Odd Fellows lodge, 1895. *(Courtesy Buchanan District Library)*

ODD FELLOWS, JUNE 20, 1909.

Odd Fellows parade heads down Front Street, June 20, 1909. Parading in the fraternal regalia helped build public awareness and support for the organization. *(Courtesy Buchanan District Library)*

Buchanan's Odd Fellows lodge staged a fierce, but good-natured, contest with their town's Benevolent and Protective Order of Elks, ca. 1910. *(Courtesy Buchanan District Library)*

The meeting hall of the Modern Woodmen of America in Buchanan, 1895. The MWA was founded in 1883 in Lyons, Iowa, as a fraternal society that would pay benefits to members' families after the death of a breadwinner. The MWA continues to the present time. *(Courtesy Buchanan District Library)*

The Modern Woodmen of America form up on West Front Street, complete with uniforms and axes, June 2, 1907. Fraternal orders like the M. W. A. gave their members a measure of economic security and also served as an opportunity for socializing. *(Courtesy Buchanan District Library)*

The Modern Woodmen of America place their axes on the street during Decoration Day festivities, June 2, 1907. Although it appears that the Woodmen are preparing for a foot race, they are probably engaged in a drill activity. *(Courtesy Buchanan District Library)*

The Modern Woodmen of America band leads the way to Oak Ridge Cemetery for Decoration Day, June 7, 1908. The Grand Army of the Republic established Decoration Day in 1868. GAR commander Gen. John A. Logan set May 30 as the day for laying flowers on the graves of war dead. The day became Memorial Day in 1882 to honor the fallen of all wars. In 1971, Congress set Memorial Day as a national holiday on the last Monday in May. *(Courtesy Buchanan District Library)*

Buchanan staged a huge homecoming celebration in September 1910, complete with parade. This float celebrates town blacksmith Elmer E. Remington, who apparently demonstrated his trade as he rode along. *(Courtesy Buchanan District Library)*

The float for D. L. Boardman's shop in the 1910 homecoming parade proudly announced the "Adjusto Corset for Stout Women," and even displayed a few examples on forms. Ruth Reese Marsh, appearing relatively slender, is seated second from right. *(Courtesy Buchanan District Library)*

Parade down Front Street during Buchanan's Homecoming celebration in 1910. *(Courtesy Buchanan District Library)*

A marching band heads down Front Street, ca. 1910. *(Courtesy Buchanan District Library)*

Children as well as adults participated in parades. These girls are ready with their strollers for a "Doll Parade" during Buchanan's Harvest Jubilee, September 25-28, 1912. *(Courtesy Buchanan District Library)*

A rather crude wagon advertises tintype photographs at a studio on Days Avenue for the 4th of July, 1908. Like the wagon, tintypes were antiquated by 1908 – the advertising may have been a jest. *(Courtesy Buchanan District Library)*

The Ferris Wheel debuted at the Columbian Exposition in Chicago in 1893.
American engineer George Ferris designed the original massive wheel to outdo
the Eiffel Tower in Paris. The 250-foot diameter wheel carried 2,160 passengers at a time and made such a hit with the public that other operators tried
to emulate its success. This one is getting ready to carry passengers aloft in
Buchanan, ca. 1910. *(Courtesy Buchanan District Library)*

Buchanan's homecoming celebration in 1910 featured a balloon ascension.
The balloon rises into the sky behind the old Advent Church on Oak Street.
(Courtesy Buchanan District Library)

An early marching band, probably for the Civil War veterans' organization, the Grand Army of the Republic, ca. 1875. Some of the brass instruments are fashioned to point the bell over the musician's shoulder so the sound carries to marchers following behind. John Morris is seated in center front, with James Harvey Roe standing at far right. *(Courtesy Buchanan District Library)*

Another early marching band, ca. 1870. Alison C. Roe is seated at left. *(Courtesy Buchanan District Library)*

Merton L. Hanlin of Clark Equipment Company (right, in straw boater) with a band from the Israelite House of David, 1910. The House of David, a communal religious order founded in Benton Harbor in 1903, boasted many members with musical talent. Its jazz band, in particular, toured nationally. Among its religious tenets was the belief that men should not shave or cut their hair. The long-haired children in this photograph are boys, not girls. *(Courtesy Buchanan District Library)*

The Buchanan Cornet Band, 1904. *(Courtesy Buchanan District Library)*

The Buchanan Concert Band, ca. 1905. *(Courtesy Dale E. Florey Collection)*

The Buchanan Cornet Band, 1909. Nearly every town in the region had a cornet band that entertained on the 4th of July and other public festivals. *(Courtesy Buchanan District Library)*

The Buchanan Concert Band ready for a performance, ca. 1915. Left to right: Fred Mead, Leland Cassler, Jake Rough, Jack Kenyon, Gene Halleck, Billie Wood. *(Courtesy Buchanan District Library)*

The band for Buchanan's American Legion Post No. 51, ca. 1925. *(Courtesy Buchanan District Library)*

Veterans of the Civil War and World War I line up in front of the Buchanan fire hall for Decoration Day, May 30, 1919. The WW I veterans are unidentified, but the elderly Civil War veterans are, left to right: Henry Rundell, Raymond Broceus, Sol Wirick, John Curtis, Steven Scott, Ashbury Rose, Theodore W. Thomas, Hoel C. Wright, Charles E. Sabin, Ashley Carlisle, George Hanley, Robert Graham, unknown, Oscar Richmond, Newton Batchelor, John Dick, Marion Huff, Sam Bunker, Omar Tabor and William Conrad. *(Courtesy Buchanan District Library)*

Farmer's Dinner at the Buchanan school, August 23, 1913. *(Courtesy Buchanan District Library)*

The Blossomtime Festival originated in St. Joseph/Benton Harbor in 1906 to promote the area's fruit industry to tourists. Its activities, including a community queen contest, soon expanded to other towns. Cecelia Eisenhart took the crown of both Miss Buchanan and Miss Blossomtime in 1930. *(Courtesy Buchanan District Library)*

WLS Radio in Chicago broadcast from rural communities throughout the region on its "Barn Dance" program. This one aired from the Buchanan High School auditorium, October 10-12, 1935. Rural programming was important to WLS, as the Sears, Roebuck Company owned the station. Sears mail order catalogs brought big city shopping to rural America. The radio station's call letters, WLS, stood for the Sears motto, "World's Largest Store." Dale E. Florey is the little boy in front with banjo. *(Courtesy Buchanan District Library)*

Dale E. Florey with his banjo, about age 6.
(Dale E. Florey Collection)

Children in 18th century costumes, possibly for a 4th of July program. Left to right: Dode Portz, Alfred Roe, Cleo Portz and Lee Roe. *(Courtesy Buchanan District Library)*

Oscar Morris (a telephone electrician); Phay Graffort (movie theater owner); and Tennyson E. Van Every (a postal worker) in costume for some now forgotten drama or lodge function, ca. 1915. *(Courtesy Buchanan District Library)*

Buchanan High School Boys' Basketball Team, 1905-1906. Left to right: Ebern Geyer, Ward Hamilton, "Sport" Broceus, Charles Baer, Elmer Ray. Dr. James Naismith invented the game of basketball at the YMCA in Springfield, Massachusetts, in 1891 to provide an indoor game during the winter. Players initially used a soccer ball that they tossed at two peach baskets. *(Courtesy Buchanan District Library)*

The Buchanan High School Girls' Basketball Team, 1906-1907. Girls' basketball originated at Smith College in 1892, where the schools' first physical education director, Senda Berenson Abbott, started a team. Abbott's rules confined each player to a third of the court. *(Courtesy Buchanan District Library)*

Basketball game in progress, ca. 1940. Reamer's Market sponsored one of the teams. *(Courtesy Buchanan District Library)*

Buchanan High School basketball team, 1939-1940. *(Courtesy Buchanan District Library)*

The Atlas Belting Co. baseball team. Ted Rouse is in front wearing a white shirt. Many companies sponsored baseball teams for their advertising value. Good players went on the company payroll less for their value as workers than for their talent on the diamond. *(Courtesy Buchanan District Library)*

The town's premier baseball team, the Buchanan Blues, ca. 1920. *(Courtesy Buchanan District Library)*

A rare photograph of a baseball game in progress, ca. 1915. *(Courtesy Buchanan District Library)*

DARBY PHOTO.

BUCHANAN BLUES
1911

1-HARRY-BEERY	7-TED-ROUSE
2-BUN-BALDWIN	8-DAN-MERSON
3-CRESS-WELDON	9-CAP-ASHBY
4-CHAS-ROUSE	10-MAGGIE-VAHLERT
5-LA RUE-MILLER	11-EARL-DUNKELBERGE
6-CLYDE-TREAT.	12-GUY-BRUCE
	13-KENNETH-PETER'S

The Buchanan Blues baseball team ranked among the region's best ball clubs. Seen here in 1911 are, back row: Harry Beery, Bun Baldwin, Cresse Weldon (in black), Charles Rouse, LaRue Miller; center row: Clyde Treat, Ted Rouse (in white fedora), Maggie Vahlert (in front of Rouse), Dan Merson, Cap Ashby; front row: Earl Dunkleberger, Guy Bruce, Kenneth Peters. *(Courtesy Buchanan District Library)*

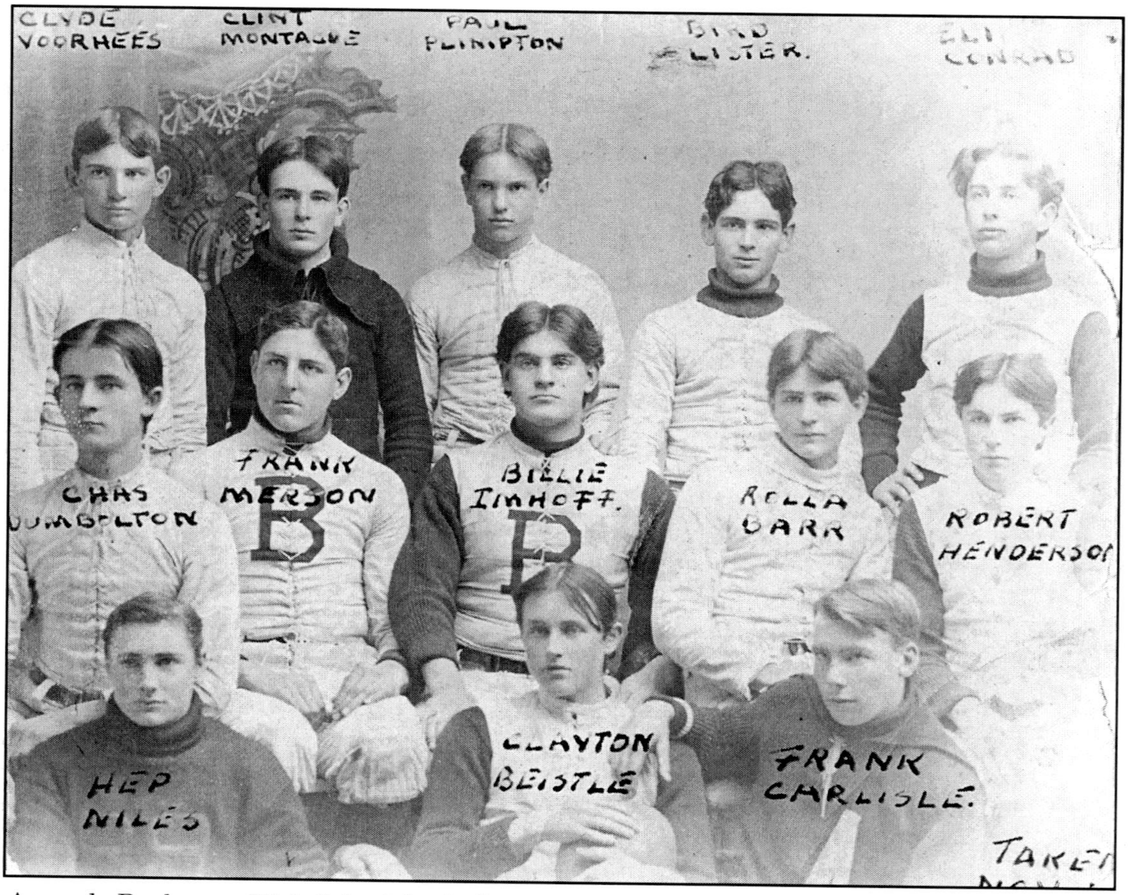

An early Buchanan High School football team, 1876. Front row: Hep Niles, Clayton Beistle, Frank Carlisle. Middle row: Charles Dumbolton, Frank Merson, Billie Imhoff, Rolla Barr, Robert Henderson. Back row: Clyde Voorhees, Clint Montague, Paul Plimpton, Bird Lister, Eli Conrad. Football originated in England in the mid-19th century and soon became popular in America. Harvard and Yale Universities met in 1876 to formalize the game's rules, which was then essentially an American form of rugby. Rule changes in the early 1880s created the game as it is known today. *(Courtesy Buchanan District Library)*

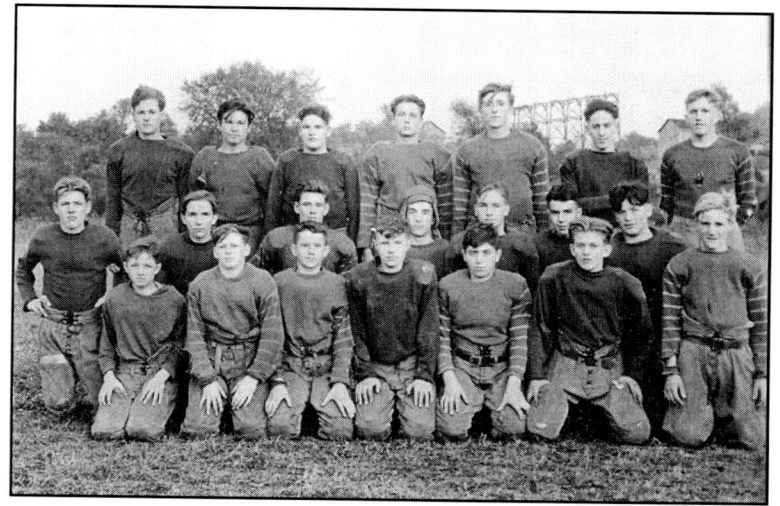

The Buchanan High School football team, 1930. *(Courtesy Buchanan District Library)*

Orchard Hills Golf Course on the Niles-Buchanan Road, ca. 1920. *(Courtesy Buchanan District Library)*

Orchard Hills Golf Course. The golf course originated as a nine-hole golf course around 1918. *(Courtesy Buchanan District Library)*

This group of
Buchananites
went to visit
Mammoth Cave
in Kentucky,
ca. 1910.
Already a major
tourist attrac-
tion, Mammoth
Cave still
lacked easily
accessible paths
- note the
visitor's sturdy
clothing for
their spelunk-
ing adventure.
*(Courtesy
Buchanan
District Li-
brary)*

Members of the Chicago Buchanan Society at Jackson Park in Chicago, 1913. This was
apparently a group of Buchanan expatriates living in Chicago. *(Courtesy Buchanan District
Library)*

Chapter 12
Famous Buchananites

John D. Ross

Many Americans in the nineteenth century spent much of their lives coping with personal tragedy. Few, however, endured so much loss as one of Buchanan's most prominent citizens, John D. Ross.

John Ross was born on January 2, 1802, in Trumbull City, Ohio. As a young man living in Cincinnati, he learned the blacksmithing trade. He married Elizabeth Labertan in 1824 and moved to New Castle, Indiana, with his young bride. John and Elizabeth had six children, but in 1832 a cholera epidemic swept through the Midwest. Soldiers from New York, sent to fight the Sauk Indians in the Black Hawk War, had brought the disease with them. John Ross watched helplessly as Elizabeth and five of their children died; only his youngest child, Thomas, survived.

In 1834, John Ross and Thomas moved to Niles, Michigan. After four years in Niles, he moved to Hudson Lake, where he met and married his second wife, Jane Conner.

The Ross & Alexander brick block on West Front Street, 1860. *(Map of the Counties Cass, Van Buren and Berrien, 1860)*

[288]

He and his new wife moved to Indiana, where he ran a dry goods store, but in 1838 a wave of ague struck. A form of malaria, ague was commonplace in the swampy lands of Michigan and northern Indiana. Jane and one child died. John Ross married for a third time on May 2, 1839, to Martha A. DeArmond. They had three children and watched two of them die.

Ross moved to Buchanan in 1847, perhaps hoping to put all of the tragedy behind him. He invested $9,000 in the purchase of five acres of land on the south side of Front Street. He had the foresight to see that Buchanan would develop in that direction and the value of his land would skyrocket, although he later noted that the only buildings then standing on that side of the street consisted of a house, a mill and a distillery. He first opened a general store, which also became the post office when Ross was appointed Buchanan's first postmaster in 1848. Running a general store while also serving a postmaster did not tax Ross's abilities, for the volume of mail was quite small. The high cost of postage in those early days of postal service prevented most people from sending letters. In 1852, for example, a correspondent could mail a letter written on a single sheet of paper a distance of up to forty miles for six to eight cents. The postmaster did not deliver the mail himself. Instead, recipients had to call at the post office and ask for their letters. On occasion, postmasters would advertise the names of people in their town who had letters waiting for them.

For a short time, the postal service allowed people to send letters cash on delivery. Instead of the sender paying for a stamp when he mailed the letter, the recipient would pay when it arrived. Unfortunately, people soon discovered that they could write a message on the back of the letter. The recipient would read the message, which contained all the information he desired, and then refuse to pay for its delivery. The postal system soon discontinued COD letters.

Besides serving as postmaster in Buchanan, John Ross also worked as a banker. He and Thomas M. Fulton opened a private bank at Buchanan in 1852, and in 1869 bought out the banking interest of George M. Colby in Niles. Ross ran the bank in Buchanan while Fulton saw to the business in Niles. In September 1872, Fulton having returned to Buchanan, the bank became the First National Bank of Buchanan. Fulton served as the bank's president and Ross's son, A. F. Ross, worked as the cashier, while John Ross himself was one of the bank directors. On December 31, 1873, the bank again became a private bank under the name of J. D. Ross & Son.

Always interested in seeing Buchanan grow, John Ross platted Ross's Addition to Buchanan on the south side of town, and then platted three more additions with fellow businessman Lorenzo P. Alexander; today, hundreds of people still live in homes in Ross's various additions. Ross won election to the Michigan Legislature in 1854 as the Democratic party candidate, was elected village president in 1859 and reelected eight times more, and ran a flour mill in town. In 1856, Ross bought land at the corner of West Front and South Oak Streets in Buchanan, where he built a beautiful Greek Revival style house. The house still stands in Buchanan, best known recently as the Buchanan Police Station.

Having married three times, and buried two wives and nine children, John Ross died in Buchanan on April 7, 1888, at age 86. He rests today beside his third wife, Martha, and his children in Buchanan's Oak Ridge Cemetery.

Hannah Carlisle

When Abraham Lincoln called for volunteers for the Union army, Hannah Carlisle answered.

Patriotism ran deep in Buchanan during the American Civil War. Scores of Buchanan men served in the federal army, fighting to restore the Union and end slavery. Townswomen supported the war effort as well. They sent clothing, blankets and food to family members and friends in the army. They also tended to farms and businesses at home while their husbands were away. One woman, Hannah Carlisle, could not bear to stay home. Leaving her elderly husband behind, Hannah left home to serve through the war as an army nurse.

Hannah Lewis Glover was born in Phelps, New York, on April 22, 1823. Her sister Louisa, her elder by 22 years, had married Daniel Carlisle, a New Hampshireman who had moved to the Phelps area. Hannah moved to Cassopolis in 1850. Louisa Carlisle had died, and on July 11, 1852, the 54 year-old Daniel married his 29 year-old sister-in-law. Although such May-December romances might raise eyebrows in more recent years, marriages between in-laws such as Daniel and Hannah were not uncommon in the nineteenth century.

When Southern secession turned into open warfare after the attack on Fort Sumter in April 1861, hundreds of thousands of Northern men rushed to enlist in the army. In the intensely patriotic Carlisle household, Daniel's age of 63 years and ill health prevented him from enlisting. Two sons from his first marriage, however, joined the Union army. Isaac and Orville Carlisle both served in Company L of the 2nd Michigan Cavalry. Hannah also wanted to contribute to the war effort and volunteered for service as an army nurse.

Hannah left Buchanan with her stepsons' regiment on November 14, 1861, for St. Louis, Missouri, where the army assigned her to the regimental hospital. Hannah served there as a hospital nurse until February 1862, when the 2nd Michigan received orders to move to Fort Donelson. Hannah went home to Buchanan. A few months later, on the evening of July 14, 1862, Hannah received a telegram from the United States Sanitary Commission asking her to report for duty in Chicago the next day. She immediately packed her bags, bade her family a hasty good-bye, and set off. In Chicago, Hannah was soon ordered to report to Post Hospital No. 1 in Columbus, Kentucky.

Hannah's absence left a void at home. Daniel apparently supported her decision to serve, but wrote in a somewhat backhanded reassurance that, "We get Along Comfortably except Want of means To Live on But you could not remidy that." Disaster struck the family on October 31, 1862, when a devastating fire in Buchanan spread to the Carlisle farm. Hannah's stepdaughter Mary wrote, "Our house, barn and all (with many other buildings) was yesterday burned to the ground." The family lost most of their possessions in the fire and had to rent a cottage in town. In a letter home, Hannah replied that, "All must look dark," but declared stoically, "We must bear it the best we can under the circumstances."

Hannah kept busy caring for sick men in the hospital. Disease, not combat, accounted for about two-thirds of the fatalities among soldiers during the Civil War. The soldiers fell ill with pneumonia, typhoid fever, dysentery, diarrhea and smallpox. Sick men often filled the post hospital wards, and the doctors and patients alike welcomed a woman's care. When Hannah came back to the hospital after a brief visit home in the summer of 1863, the doctor in charge expressed his gratitude at her return. The sick men, he said, had needed proper nourishment, but the unskilled and careless cooks had often served food that was either half-cooked or burned.

Hannah's six year-old daughter, Arabella, accompanied her to the hospital. "Belle," whom her mother described as "a sun beam . . . flitting in every direction," delighted the patients. The soldiers missed their own families, and Belle provided them with a sense of he little girl befriended a young army captain who was recovering from rheumatism and walked with the aid of crutches. He loaned Belle a crutch as a make-believe weapon and the two fought spirited duels. The captain, who pretended to be a rebel, ended up with bruised shins and had to swear allegiance to the Union before his playmate would relinquish her armament.

 Hannah worked at the post hospital until the war ended. She afterward entered the Western Department of the Freedman's-Aid Commission and returned to Columbus, where for a year she taught in a school for freed slaves. Besides helping teach over 120 students, her duties apparently included handling much of the school's administrative work. In March 1866, she wrote to Daniel that she her time was fully occupied with "Six hours in School then all the business of the commission," including answering correspondence and inventorying supplies. Nor was she safe from danger. Many ex-Confederates despised the Freedman's Bureau and attacked African-Americans and those who tried to help them. Hannah described one incident in which "ruffians" had burned a black woman's house and possessions and then nearly beaten her to death. Some of Hannah's friends in the occupying military regiments warned her to leave the region for her own safety, "But I said no, that the wicked fleeth when no man pursueth, I would not go untill forsed to do so."

 After spending a year at the school in Columbus, Hannah returned home. Her family welcomed her back to Buchanan on July 3, 1866, where she lived for the rest of her life. On February 17, 1906, she died at the home of her daughter, Arabella Osborn, in Council Bluffs, Iowa.

Hannah and Daniel Carlisle about the time of the Civil War. *(Courtesy Carlisle family, Bentley Historical Library, University of Michigan)*

Joseph Coveney

In all of its three hundred year history, Berrien County has never seen a more eccentric individual than Joseph Coveney. Coveney, a Buchanan resident, baffled people for more than sixty years with the contrast between his open-handed generosity and his intense anti-religious beliefs. He is best known today for the massive marker he installed in Buchanan's Oak Ridge Cemetery, a marker that proclaimed Coveney's curious theological views.

Coveney was born in 1805 in County Cork, Ireland, a country caught up in a continual struggle for religious supremacy. Although trained as a weaver, Coveney took up the carpenter's trade when he immigrated to America. There he was greatly inspired by the writings of Thomas Paine and Robert Ingersoll and became, like them, a Freethinker, espousing logic and reason over religious traditions.

Coveney worked in Pennsylvania for a short time before traveling to South Bend, Indiana, in 1833. There he married Louise Roe, the eldest daughter of local minister William Roe; the young couple soon bought property and built a house northwest of Buchanan. Coveney prospered in Buchanan, building houses and purchasing more land, and became moderately wealthy. At the same time, he was adamantly opposed to Christianity, and to twit his neighbors drove a team of horses he had named "Jesus" and "Christ."

He was also fond of expressing his theological views in no uncertain terms whenever he could find someone who would listen. One occasion came about when local attorney Albert A. Worthington, a well-known Sunday School teacher and son of a Methodist minister, met Coveney while on the road one day. Coveney was doing some road repairs, and was ready to install a new culvert when Worthington came down the road in his horse-drawn buggy.

"Mr. Worthington," said Coveney, "It will be a pleasure to put this culvert in, but first I want you to get out and sit down and discuss religion with me for half an hour."

Joseph Coveney and his wife, Louisa. *(History of Berrien and Van Buren Counties, Michigan,* 1880)

Worthington had no intention of entering into a fruitless religious debate and protested that he was too busy, but Coveney remained adamant. Neither man would give an inch, so Worthington finally made a four-mile detour around Coveney and his culvert.

Still, everyone who knew Coveney agreed that no one in the county was more generous to his fellow citizens. When the school board declared that it could afford only half the salary requested by a rural schoolteacher, Coveney offered to pay the other half out of his own pocket. He did it, too, and gave the teacher free room and board as well. His generosity, in fact, was at least as renowned as his theology, and few men were as well liked as Joseph Coveney.

Buchanan residents were delighted at the news that Coveney intended to install a three thousand dollar memorial in Oak Ridge Cemetery. Such a large monument would be a fine addition to the grounds, and Coveney was allocated a choice space in the Soldier's Plot. When the monument was unveiled in September 1874, however, people were aghast at what they saw. Inscribed on all four sides of the memorial were such sentiments as "The more priests the more poverty," "The more religion the more lying," and "All Christian denominations preach damnation to the others." The monument created an enormous outcry in Buchanan, which must have overjoyed Coveney. The memorial was smeared with red chalk, defaced, and even spat upon, but it was allowed to remain in the cemetery.

In February 1897 Coveney went to his grave unrepentant, his deathbed surrounded by pictures of Satan and various anti-Christian motifs. His memorial still stands in Oak Ridge Cemetery, a tribute to Joseph Coveney, Berrien County's most enigmatic eccentric.

The Joseph Coveney farm in Buchanan Township. *(Map of the Counties Cass, Van Buren and Berrien, Michigan,* 1860)

Jack Knight

Mail pilot Jack Knight peered down from his open-cockpit biplane at the Platt River 2,200 feet below. It was the night of February 22-23, 1921, and Jack Knight had to get the U. S. mail through.

James H. "Jack" Knight was born in Kansas on March 14, 1892, and as a small boy moved to Buchanan with his parents. He joined the Army air service in 1917 during World War I and learned to fly at Ellington Field in Houston, Texas. He remained there until the war ended, teaching advanced aerobatics to student pilots, then began flying airmail in 1919.

The Post Office Department had initiated around-the-clock relay airmail service between New York and San Francisco, with two planes flying east and two flying west. Airplanes then had no radio navigation aids, so people on the ground would light bonfires to guide the pilots. The planes would land every two hundred to three hundred miles to refuel and change pilots. Pilot Farr Nutter took off from San Francisco at 4:29 on the morning of February 22 and flew the mail to Reno. From Reno, other pilots flew to Salt Lake City and Cheyenne, Wyoming. Frank Yager flew the mail from Cheyenne to North Platte, Nebraska, landing a few minutes before 8:00 p.m.

Jack Knight, who had already made his regular run from Omaha to Cheyenne, flew back to North Platte to meet Yager. The airplane, a single-engine DeHavilland DH-4 converted from its original use as a World War I bomber, needed almost three hours of repair work, but at 10:44 that evening Jack Knight took off for Omaha. He touched down at Omaha at 1:10 in the morning to hand the mail off to his relief pilot, but the relief pilot was still in Chicago, socked in by poor weather.

Knight was exhausted. He had never flown the Omaha to Chicago route, and the weather was indeed miserable. The plane had no navigational equipment except a compass and an old railroad map, and there would be no bonfires on the ground to serve as guideposts. One of the eastbound mail planes had crashed, killing its pilot. Airport manager Bill Votaw told Knight to forget it. Most pilots would have agreed. But Jack Knight knew that the future of airmail service was riding on his flight. He asked for coffee, and then climbed back into his airplane.

He flew across Nebraska in bitter cold, using a flashlight to follow the map. He got to Des Moines, Iowa, but found the snow to deep to land; low on fuel, Knight headed for Iowa City. Somehow, he made it. The ground crew had gone home, thinking the flight was cancelled, but a watchman lit a flare that helped Knight land safely. His engine's roar brought out

Jack Knight in athe cockpit of a DH-4.
(Courtesy Buchanan District Library)

the sleepy ground crew, who refueled the plane. Knight wolfed down a ham sandwich and took off again for Chicago. When he landed in the Windy City at 8:40 that morning, his engine running on fumes, Jack Knight became an instant hero.

Jack Knight went on to set other records. He broke the U. S. Mail record in 1926 by flying coast to coast in 33 ½ hours, helped establish the government's air beacon system and demonstrated the first practical system of air-ground intercommunication. He became a pilot for United Air Lines and in 1931 held a world record of 12,000 hours in the air; he retired from flying in 1937 to become United's director of public education. During World War II, Knight contracted malaria while on a trip to South America to obtain rubber for the war effort. He returned to Buchanan in poor health, and died on February 24, 1945, in Niles' Pawating Hospital. As he had requested, his ashes were scattered from an airplane over Lake Michigan. Buchanan honored Knight in 1978 with a memorial chapel in Oak Ridge Cemetery, and Knight Drive in the Samson Terrace subdivision also honors the aviator.

None of Knight's accomplishments, however, surpassed the importance of his pioneering 1921 mail flight in the dead of winter. Airmail was then a novelty beset by great problems, and President-elect Warren G. Harding had promised to cut the federal budget by canceling all airmail service. Had Jack Knight looked into the dark snow-filled sky and stayed on the ground, airmail might have died. His flight captured public imagination, and Congress agreed to continue funding airmail service. Whenever an airmail letter goes out, Americans can thank the Buchanan pilot who saved the U. S. airmail.

Jack Knight with one of United Air Lines' DC-3s in the background. *(Courtesy Buchanan District Library)*

Virgil Exner

The world of automobile styling owes a great debt to the influence of a Buchanan native. Virgil Max Exner earned worldwide renown for his innovative automobile designs.

Virgil Exner was born in Ann Arbor, Michigan, on September 24, 1909, and adopted shortly after his birth by George and Iva Exner, a young couple from Buchanan. Virgil grew up in Buchanan and graduated from Buchanan High School in 1926. His classmates voted him the class's "Worst Primper" and "Worst Gum Chewer," but also elected him class secretary. In a nod to his artistic talents, the high school yearbook *The Pines* declared "With such a pencil, such a pen, your name will be with famous men." Exner preferred the nickname "Ex" to his real name, Virgil, for he considered "Virgil" too feminine.

"Ex" went on to study art at the University of Notre Dame, but lack of money forced him to drop out in 1928. He stayed in South Bend, Indiana, however, and got a job drawing advertisements for the Studebaker auto company. A friend suggested that he show his artwork to Harley Earl at General Motors, which resulted in Earl hiring Ex to work for Pontiac's design studio. By 1934, Virgil Exner was Pontiac's chief stylist.

Exner returned to Studebaker in 1938. The famous design firm of Raymond Loewy had lured him back to South Bend. Exner worked as Studebaker's chief stylist designing the 1941 Studebaker Champion and the company's 1947, 1948 and 1949 models. In 1949, a falling out with Loewy sent him to Chrysler. Exner joined Chrysler as head of the Advance Styling Group. In the post-World War II years, critics derided Chrysler products as the stodgiest-looking of all American cars. Chrysler's president insisted that a car's roofline should be high enough for a man to wear his hat while driving. Unfortunately, Chrysler's

Virgil Exner in a "concept car" that sports his signature tail fins. *(Courtesy Dale E. Florey Collection)*

tall, boxy-looking designs were costing the company sales, and the company's directors wanted a change. Exner immediately transformed the look of Chrysler cars. His first production cars for Chrysler in 1955 included the "microphone taillight" of the Imperial and Chrysler 300 models. Exner called his low, sleek body design the "Forward Look." Two years later, in 1957, Exner introduced the design element that won him instant fame: tail fins. Tail fins epitomized automobile designs of the late 1950s and early 1960s. Exner recalled that, "We wanted to give our cars an eager, poised-for-action look which we feel is the natural and functional shape of automobiles." In June 1957, the Industrial Designers' Institute awarded Exner and his team its Gold Medal.

In 1962, however, Chrysler fired Exner, making him a scapegoat for a failed design that that the corporate directors had insisted on themselves. Exner went on to head his own industrial design firm in Birmingham, Michigan. He worked on many auto and pleasure boat design projects, and spearheaded an unsuccessful effort to revive the Duesenberg automobile. He died on December 22, 1973, at age 64. The fabulous 1950s cars at classic auto shows or tooling down a country road remain as a legacy of Virgil Exner, the designer from Buchanan who made it all possible.

Bibliography

Primary Sources

Atlas of Berrien County, Michigan. Chicago: Rand, McNally & Co., 1887.

Atlas of Berrien County, Michigan. Philadelphia: C. O. Titus, 1873.

Blackburn, Glen A., Nellie A. Robertson and Dorothy Riker, comp. and ed. *The John Tipton Papers.* 2 Vols. Indianapolis: Indiana Historical Bureau, 1942.

Clark Equipment Company. Corporate archives. Berrien County Historical Association, Berrien Springs, MI.

Clark Equipment Company. *First Fifty Years, Clark Equipment: A story of an American Manufacturing Enterprise.* Buchanan, MI: Clark Equipment Co., 1953

DeLand, Charles J., comp. *Michigan Official Directory and Legislative Manual for the Years 1921 and 1922.* N. p., n.d.

Department of Administration, comp. *Michigan Manual.* [1971-1972] N.p., n.d.

Dignan, Herman H. *Michigan Official Directory and Legislative Manual.* [1945-1946] N.p., n.d.

Dunbar, Willis F. *Michigan: A History of the Wolverine State.* Rev. and ed. by George S. May. Grand Rapids, MI: Eerdmans Publishing Co., 1980.

Farm Journal. *The Farm Journal Illustrated Rural Directory of Berrien County, Michigan.* Philadelphia: Wilmer Atkinson Company, 1917.

Fitzgerald, Frank D. *Michigan Official Directory and Legislative Manual.* [1931-1932] N.p., n.d.

Kappler, Charles J., comp. and ed. *Indian Affairs, Laws and Treaties.* 2 Vols. Washington, DC: Government Printing Office, 1904.

Map of the Counties Cass, Van Buren and Berrien, Michigan. Philadelphia: Geil, Harley & Siverd, 1860. Reprint ed., Dowagiac, MI: Cass County Historical Commission, 1983.

Martineau, Harriet. "Harriet Martineau's Travels In and Around Michigan, 1836." *Michigan History* 7 (January-April 1923): 53 and 56.

McClary, Andrew. "Don't Go To Michigan, That Land of Ills." *Michigan History* 67 (Jan./Feb. 1983).

[298]

McCoy, Isaac. *History of Baptist Indian Missions.* Washington, DC: William M. Morrison, 1840.

Michigan Central Railroad. *Headlight.* Chicago: Michigan Central Railroad, 1895.

Osmun, Gilbert R. *Official Directory and Legislative Manual of the State of Michigan for the Years 1887-88.* Lansing: Thorp & Godfrey, 1887.

Phillips, B. E. *Plus Faith Unlimited, The Story of Clark Equipment Company.* Newcomen Society in North America: New York, 1979.

Report of Judge John L. Leib to Governor of Michigan Territory Lewis Cass, November 20, 1824, in National Archives Microfilm Publications, Microcopy No. 234, "Letters Received by the Office of Indian Affairs, 1824-81," Roll 419, Michigan Superintendency, 1824-51.

Standard Atlas of Berrien County, Michigan. Chicago: Geo. A. Ogle & Co., 1903

Vaughan, Coleman C. *Michigan Official Directory and Legislative Manual for the Years 1919 and 1920.* N.p., n.d.

Secondary Sources

Buchanan Historic District Study Committee. *Buchanan: Past and Future.* Buchanan, MI: Buchanan Historic District Study Committee, 1976.

Carney, James T., ed. *Berrien Bicentennial.* Berrien County, MI: Berrien County Bicentennial Commission, 1976

Chubb, Richard. "The History of the Buchanan Hydroelectric Plant," in the *Berrien County Record,* February 1, 2001.

Clifton, James A. *The Pokagons: 1681-1981.* Lanham, MD: Rowman & Littlefield, 1984.

Cook, Barbara W. and Grafton H. *The Round Oak Stove People, and other Dowagiac, Michigan, personalties.* Niles, MI: by the authors, 2001.

Cowles, Edward B. *Directory and History of Berrien County, Michigan.* Buchanan, MI: Record Steam Printing House, 1871.

Dunbar, Willis F. *All Aboard! A History of Railroads in Michigan.* Grand Rapids, MI: William B. Eerdmans Publishing Co., 1969.

Dunbar, Willis F. and George S. May. *Michigan: A History of the Wolverine State.* Grand Rapids, MI: William B. Eerdmans Publishing Co., 1995.

Ellis, Franklin. *History of Berrien and Van Buren Counties, Michigan.* Philadelphia: D.W. Ensign & Co., 1880.

French, Robert W. *Living Together: Buchanan and Clark, 1904-1975.* N. p., 1976.

Gowans, Alan. *Styles and Types of North American Architecture.* New York: HarperCollins Publishers, 1992; reprint ed. IconEdition, 1993.

Hawes, Walter C. *The Story of Buchanan: A History.* Originally published as "The Story of Buchanan" in serial form by the *Berrien County Record*, 1951-1953. Republished as a book: Leo J. Goodsell, ed. Berrien Springs, MI: Berrien County Historical Assocation, 2004.

Myers, Robert C. *Historical Sketches of Berrien County*, Vols. 1-4. Berrien Springs: Berrien County Historical Association, 1988, 1989, 1994, 2001.

_____. "The St. Joseph Valley Railroad Company." *Michigan History* 72 (January/February 1988): 24-30.

Portrait and Biographical Record, of Berrien and Cass Counties, Michigan. Chicago: Biographical Publishing Co., 1893.

Pray, Carl E. "An Historic Michigan Road." *Michigan History* 11 (July 1927): 325-35.

Ryman, Donald F. *Buchanan's Heritage.* Buchanan, MI: Buchanan Preservation Society, 1984.

Ryman, Donald F. *The Mills on Buchanan's McCoy's Creek.* Berrien History No. 6. Berrien Springs: Berrien County Historical Association, 1984.

Satz, Ronald N. *American Indian Policy in the Jacksonian Era.* Lincoln: University of Nebraska Press, 1976.

Schultz, George A. *An Indian Canaan: Isaac McCoy and the Vision of an Indian State.* Norman: University of Oklahoma Press, 1972.

State of Michigan. *Michigan Official Directory and Legislative Manual, 1931-1932.* Lansing: State of Michigan, 1931.

Wilcox, Wayne. Correspondence with the authors, June 9, 2005.

Yeager, Randolph O. "Indian Enterprises of Isaac McCoy: 1817-1846." Ph.D. diss. Norman: University of Oklahoma Graduate College, 1954.

Internet Sources:

Kahn, Al. *Time Capsule: History of Electro-Voice.* 1953. www.prosoundweb.com/install/commentary/kc/ev/timecapsule3.shtml. 21 September 2004.

Clark, Keith. Reflections: Electro-Voice At 70 And Beyond. 2004. www.prosoundweb.com/install/commentary/kc/ev/ev.shtml. 21 September 2004.

Newspapers

Berrien County Record
Herald-Palladium
Niles Republican

Index

Sweeney, Hattie, *224*
Swem Funeral Home, *91*
Swem, Harvey, *206*

Tabor, E., *67*
Tabor, Frances, *232*
Tabor, Omar, *275*
Taylor, Dan, *206*
Terrel, Rev. Josiah, 235
Territorial Road, 129
Tees, Ted, *206*
Thayer, Frank H., *227, 228*
Thayer, Lottie, *226*
The Advent Times, 236
The Independent, 43
The Pines, 295
Theater, Buchanan's First, *278*
Thomas, John, 15
Thomas, Theodore W., *275*
Thompson, Squire, 11, 15
Thompson's I.G.A., 45
Thorpe, Stanton, *207*
Thorson, Fred, *207*
Three Oaks Catholic Church, 238
Thurston, William, *206*
Tichenor, Fred, *223*
Tichenor, Georgia, *223*
Tin Shop Theater, 45, 255
Toledo Strip, *9*
Tomlinson, Benjamin and Harriet
    (House), *102*
Tomlinson, Benjamin, *32*
Topinabe, Chief, 13, 15
Transportation, 129-155
Trapp, Frank, *207*
Treat & Redden grocery, *122*
Treat Building, *88*
Treat, Ann, *227*
Treat, Clyde, *283*
Treat, Markus, *155*
Treat, Willis, *88*
Treaty of Chicago, 12-13, 15
Tremont House Hotel, 44, *46*
Trophy House, *95*
Troutfetter, Irene, *232*
Truhn, Al, *206*
Tucek, Godfrey, *207*
Twelfth Indiana Cavalry, *115*
Tyler Refrigeration, 184

UAW-CIO, 183

Under Fire, 82
Union Block, 43
Union Knife Company, 159
Union School, see Buchan High School
United Air Lines, 294
United Auto Workers, 185
United Brethren Church, 235, 236,
    242, 243, 244
United States, 8, 11, 13, 14, 16, 17, 160
    Congress, 8, 9, 15, 129
    Government land office, 18-19
    House of Representatives, 7
    Sanitary Commission, 289
    Senate, 7, 11
    Supreme Court, 8
    Topographical Engineers, 28
    War Department, 13, 28
University of Michigan, *20, 123*
University of Notre Dame, 295
US-12, 129, 132
Utrup, Alvin, *207*
Utrup, Wilbur, *207*

Vahlert, Maggie, *283*
Valparaiso Moraine, *21*
Van Every, Tennyson E., *98, 278*
Van Meter, Maggie, *116*
Van Meter, William, *116*
Van Meter's bakery, *48*
Van Riper, Jacob J., *123*
Van Riper, Emma E., *123*
Van Riper, Jacob J. family, *123*
Vincent, Isaac M., 235
Volkers, John, *201*
Voorhees, Clyde, *284*
Votaw, Bill, 293

Wade, Gale, *207*
Wagner Road, 219
Wagner School, 218
Wagner, Daniel A., 43
Wagner, Ira, *138*
Wagner, Jane Mansfield, 217
Wagner, M., *67*
Wagner, Minta, *232*
Wales, Russ, *206*
Wallin, Dr. Charles C., 17, 157
Walls, Jacob, *211*
Walls, Lewis, *207*
War of 1812, 7, 13, 15
Warner, Joe, *206*